Contents

Acknowledgments

I express my sincere thanks to a number of special people who helped make this book possible:

To Judi Perry, for having the vision for this book and for her expert editing. We make a great team!

To Beacon Hill Press of Kansas City, for sharing my passion to help people hurting in dysfunctional relationships.

To the cover design and titling team for their awesome creativity.

To Bob Noonan, for support of my ministry and sharing his wisdom and expertise.

To my husband, daughters, family, and friends, for supporting and loving me.

To all those who have shared with me their struggles in difficult relationships and taught me in the process.

To my sponsors, Gloria and Cindy, for helping me apply these principles in my life and relationships.

To the Lord, for making all things work for good in my life for His glory. He is so faithful to His promises!

To CLASServices, for stirring my passion to write and showing me how to do it.

Introduction

Are you in a hurtful relationship with someone you love? Are you in a relationship in which you find yourself struggling to force change, give advice, control, or fix problems? This hurtful relationship can be with anyone who is important to you: a son, daughter, stepson, stepdaughter, husband, wife, parent, stepparent, brother, sister, aunt, uncle, grandparent, friend, in-law, ex-spouse, ex-spouse's partner, boyfriend, girlfriend, or anyone else who is in your life. The difficulties can stem from addiction, mental illness, abuse, a trying personality, general dysfunction, irresponsibility, or any number of other things that interfere with a healthy relationship. Regardless of the cause, you find your relationship with someone you care about is about to break under the strain.

You're in a complicated and confusing place. Your emotions run the gamut from love to hate to anger to compassion. You fear you're overreacting; but then again, maybe you're not reacting enough. You work hard at fixing things so that the one you care about suffers as little as possible—probably causing your own suffering in the process. In the end, it may seem your efforts often make things even worse, maybe preventing the very change you're seeking.

Regardless of the specific problem you're dealing with, you're affected in predictable ways. No doubt you have feelings of guilt and inadequacy. Perhaps you've been accused of being controlling and driven to make your loved one change. You probably often feel unloved, frustrated, and sad. You may have trouble taking care of yourself and your life because you're focused on the problems associated with your difficult relationship. You're trying to keep things under control by forcing change or by passive acceptance to

keep the peace or gain approval. You may find yourself reacting more than taking action.

This difficult relationship may be causing problems for
you in your other relationships. Maybe you're torn between
two family members because pleasing one hurts the other.
Perhaps disagreements over the ways you're dealing with a
loved one are splitting your marriage or family apart. It's
very possible that you know you're neglecting other relationships by focusing on this dysfunctional one.

Here are some scenarios in which you may see yourself:

- A demanding parent is causing problems in your immediate family.
- You're considering raising your grandchildren because
  their parents are unable or unwilling to do it themselves.
- Your child, sibling, or parent is mentally ill or suffers
  from an addiction and refuses to get help.
- A loved one is so irresponsible that you've taken over
  his or her life.

Obviously, I can't address every possible dysfunctional relationship in this book, but I can tell you that the *dilemmas*
created by dysfunctional relationships are always basically
the same.

The 10 principles set out in this book will help you experience freedom even in the midst of your difficulties. You
can achieve the freedom to let go and love your loved one,
to live your life and allow your loved one to live his or her
life, and to experience peace. When you're free from trying
to fix someone else's life, you'll be free to utilize the talents
God has given you to live life fully. Your difficult relationships will change—because *you* will change.

As you gain the information, insights, and principles set
out in this book, you can apply them to your situation as
they work for you. You may choose to implement the principles gradually, or you may find that you would benefit from
professional counseling.

This is not a quick-fix process. Some of the principles will seem too difficult for you to incorporate into your life right away. You'll grow into them. One thing is certain, though: Your difficult relationship will stay the same or worsen if you continue to do what you've been doing up to now. As you apply these principles to your situation, you'll begin to change and heal, increasing the chances that your difficult loved one and your relationship with him or her will change and improve.

UNDERSTAND SCRIPTURAL TRUTHS

Do your best to present yourself to God as one approved, a workman who does not need to be ashamed and who correctly handles the word of truth.
                                                        —2 Tim. 2:15

I f you're struggling in a relationship that has become dysfunctional, as a Christian you may be asking yourself what God wants you to do. It seems peace is unattainable. You pray, but you still worry and react. You wonder why God doesn't answer your prayers or even seem to care that your heart is breaking. Your loved one may even use your faith manipulatively by calling you a hypocrite in an effort to get you to do what he or she wants, saying, "A good Christian wouldn't do that."

It's therefore important that you understand the scriptural truths that give you a firm foundation on which to stand. Jesus spent time with difficult people, and He loved them.

God values relationship so much that He created us to have relationship with Him. When we became *difficult* by choosing again and again to sin, He cared enough to come after us, pursuing us with a love so great that He sacrificed His only Son.

He also wants us to have good relationships with others. Much of the New Testament was written to individuals and local churches about how relationships should be conducted. The fruit of the Spirit—love, joy, peace, patience, kindness, goodness, faithfulness, gentleness, and self-control—

are all qualities that enhance relationships (Gal. 5:22-23).
The hardest place to live your faith is in the context of relationships with sinful, broken people, but that's precisely
what God wants you to do. Your love for God can best be
measured by your love for others (1 John 4:7-21).

WHAT IS CHRISTIAN LOVE?

Phil's wife is having an affair. She left him to care for
their three children on his own. Phil wants his wife back,
and he believes that loving her means he must continue to
take care of her needs while she's living with another man,
all the while praying that she'll come back home.

Joan and Ron continue to support their son, who is on
drugs. They're afraid that if they cut off his money, he'll feel
unloved and get worse.

Rita and John disapprove of their daughter's decision to
marry Brad. Since she continues to stay with him in spite of
his alcoholism and abuse, they won't have anything to do
with either one of them.

Each of these situations exemplifies a misunderstanding
of love. As Christians, we sometimes misapply the Bible because we have a tendency to look at truth too simplistically.
We surmise that if love means never showing disapproval,
then that's all it means. Or if love suffers long, then it
means to hold on no matter what. If love means to confront
sin, then it must be harsh and confrontational. We tend to
ignore the fullness of God's truth by not recognizing that
love is multifaceted.

Love Is Treating Your Neighbor as Yourself

Jesus commanded you to love others as yourself (Matt.
22:37-39). In practice, this requires you to put the other
person in a higher position than yourself. It's the opposite
of selfishness or self-centeredness. If an action would benefit you but hurt another, it's clear that you're to put the

good of others first. "Do to others as you would have them do to you" (Luke 6:31) means that you love by treating others at least as well as you treat yourself. If you're unsure, measure your actions by how you would like to be treated. Love is not dependent on feeling affection; it's an act of the *will*, in which you choose to put another's best interest ahead of your own.

This does not mean that taking care of yourself is prohibited, however. "Make every effort to do what leads to peace and to *mutual* edification" (Rom. 14:19, emphasis added). It's not in the best interest of the other person to allow him or her to mistreat you. Phil. 2:4 says, "Each of you should look not only to your own interests, but also to the interests of others." You're responsible primarily for yourself. You must attend to your interests in order to do that.

"Love does no harm to its neighbor" (Rom. 13:10). You harm others when you enable them to do things that hurt themselves or others—including you. It's hurtful to your loved one if you financially support irresponsible and destructive behaviors, cover sin, or react in ways that are emotionally damaging.

Love Is Unconditional

The ultimate standard is to love as Christ loved us (John 15:12). Christ's love is permanent, unchanging, and unconditional (Rom. 8:35-39).

God showed us this love by sending His Son to die for us (Rom. 5:8). We show unconditional love to others when we treat them lovingly for who they are, valuable children of God, not because of what they do or don't do. Paul showed unconditional love toward the Corinthians even when it was not returned (2 Cor. 6:12). This means that no matter what your loved one does, you continue to act in ways that show love. You can love your loved one while hating the sin that enslaves, controls, rules, and destroys.

The confusion surrounding unconditional love is that it's often confused with approval. It's possible to show disapproval without withholding love, and it's possible to love without approving. In fact, showing disapproval can sometimes be the most loving thing you can do.

Love Is Compassionate Toughness

Having compassion means you have sympathy and feel sorry about the difficulty your loved one is encountering even if it's a result of his or her choices. The words "mercy" and "compassion" are often used interchangeably. "Compassion" and "kindness" are often found together. They're the opposite of a judgmental or condemning spirit. Rom. 2:4 tells us that it's God's kindness, not harsh judgment, that leads to repentance.

God has compassion toward us. When the Israelites suffered as slaves in Egypt, they cried out to God. Exod. 2:24 says, "God *heard* their groaning and he *remembered* his covenant with Abraham, with Isaac and with Jacob. So God *looked* on the Israelites and was *concerned* about them" (emphasis added). He said, "I have indeed seen the misery of my people. . . . I have heard them crying out . . . and I am concerned about their suffering. So I have come down to rescue them" (Exod. 3:7-8). God *cares*—even when suffering is the result of sin.

As there is a time for compassion and mercy, there is also a time for tough love. Tough love is love that makes it possible for you to allow your loved one to suffer in the hope that he or she will be saved. Tough love allows you to draw boundaries, to speak the truth in love, to say no, and to allow consequences. Tough love is not administered in anger but out of a deep understanding of the needs of the person and a concern for his or her long-term well-being.

Compassionate toughness confronts without destroying. Paul confronted the Early Church with its sin. He said, "I wrote you out of great distress and anguish of heart and with many tears, not to grieve you but to let you know the depth of my love for you" (2 Cor. 2:4). He says of one particular man that the punishment he received was enough so that now he should be forgiven "so that he will not be overwhelmed by excessive sorrow. I urge you, therefore, to reaffirm your love for him" (2 Cor. 2:7-8).

Jesus treated sinners with heartfelt compassion. The Pharisees refused to have relationships with difficult people, but Jesus went to them, and as a result, they believed His message (Luke 7:29-30). The Pharisees brought an adulterous woman to Jesus (John 8:2-11). Jesus refused to condemn her, instead telling her to leave her sinful life. He forgave it without excusing it while expecting her to change direction. Jesus spoke kindly to the divorced Samaritan woman living in adultery (John 4:4-26). If Jesus were on earth today, He would go first to the difficult people: the addicts, the emotionally wounded, the mentally ill, and the sexually immoral.

Love Is Severing a Relationship Only When Necessary

There are times when a relationship must be broken—but as a last resort and for serious situations only. Paul occasionally exhorted the church to expel a member for persistent and unrepentant sin, but it was to be done in a way that treated him or her like a brother or sister rather than an enemy with the hope it would produce repentance and restoration (2 Thess. 3:13-15; 1 Cor. 5:1-13).

Defending yourself and your family by cutting off extremely dangerous or destructive relationships is permissible. Jesus withdrew himself repeatedly from men who were trying to harm Him (John 7:30; Luke 4:30).

However, you would not want to sever a relationship to show disapproval of what the person is doing, to manipulatively get your own way, or to communicate a threat. Main-

taining a relationship in which you can love unconditionally
and be an influence for good is the right alternative in all
but extreme situations. Many broken, wounded people have
said that they first felt God's love through the unconditional
love of a spouse or family member.

Love Is Seeking Reconciliation When Possible

Reconciliation is the highest goal. God desires unity and
peace whenever possible (Rom. 12:18), but it takes two people who want to work toward restoring honesty, trust, mutual concern, and respect to restore a broken relationship.

You may have family members or friends with whom you
have a broken relationship. If you would like to reestablish
that relationship, initiate contact in a small way, such as via a
phone call, a card, or an E-mail. Reconciliation cannot take
place unless the other person wants it also, of course, and
that will happen only when he or she is ready. You can let
your loved one know that you want a restored relationship.
Your responsibility is to keep the door open.

Love Is Custom-ordered

A loving act to one person may be enabling or insulting
to another. For instance, it may be insulting to one daughter for you to make inquiries regarding her college education because she perceives your questions as an indication
that you don't trust her ability to do it right. A different
daughter may welcome your concern as a loving gesture,
viewing your willingness to spend time on her as positive
and helpful. Take your loved one's circumstances, personality, and perceptions into consideration. True love discovers
the needs and adapts itself to them.

Love Is Willing to Say No

"Submit to one another out of reverence for Christ.
Wives, submit to your husbands as to the Lord" (Eph. 5:21-
22). In these verses submission infers subordinating your

needs to act in the best interest of the other. Both persons in a relationship should act in this manner toward each other.

God has established order within the home. The husband is the head of the family in a structural way. Someone has to be in charge when there are impasses; however, that does not imply that the wife is unimportant or unable to fully participate in decisions, nor that the husband rules like a dictator. Decisions should always be agreed upon, when possible, in a cooperating partnership that values both individuals equally. The wife submits to her husband by respecting him, loving him, and honoring him, as long as it does not require her to violate her conscience or God's Word. The husband should also submit to his wife in the context of loving and caring for her as his own body, as long as it does not violate his conscience and his responsibility to act in a way that increases her holiness (Eph. 5:25-29).

Submission is always voluntary and can be withheld. Each individual has control over his or her life. Submission is not the same as obedience. Obedience implies a parent-child relationship (Eph. 6:1). A husband-wife relationship is based on love and mutual respect, not obedience. Each has a responsibility to bring insights, talents, and varying viewpoints into the relationship, including the ability to say no. Adult children are no longer under the authority of the parents; however, parents have the right to set rules for their household, as do adult children for theirs.

As you deal with your difficult loved one, there are times you'll have to do what you believe is right, even if it's not what others want you to do. But remember—you have to live with yourself. You must follow your conscience.

Paul tells us to submit to authorities in government (Rom. 13:1-7) unless the government's orders go against God's commands. Peter was told by the authorities not to preach Christ, and he refused to obey, stating, "We must obey God rather than men" (Acts 5:29). The apostle Paul was thrown into jail

many times for disobeying the law by preaching. Hebrew
midwives refused the king of Egypt's command to kill baby
boys (Exod. 1:15-21). For the higher good of saving her people from death, Queen Esther disobeyed her husband by
speaking against his edict to kill Jews (Esther 5). Abigail disobeyed her husband to save lives by bringing David and his
men the provisions Nabal refused them (1 Sam. 25). Following righteousness *always* comes before submission.

Consider these modern examples:

- Maggie continued to have a relationship with her son
  in prison even though her husband had forbidden her
  to see him.
- Jackie stayed by her sister's side even though the rest
  of the family disowned Jill because of the man she
  married and the lifestyle they lived.
- Rick continued to have a relationship with his brother
  even though Rick's wife got angry.
- Megan helped pay for treatment of her daughter's
  mental illness even though her husband refused to admit she suffered from one.
- Jared continued a relationship with his adult children
  from his prior marriage even though his new wife was
  jealous and didn't want him to.
- Peter's family got angry when he refused to give money to pay for his brother's bail, but he stood firm.

When it's a matter of standing up for good, standing
against wrong, following your conscience, and protecting
others and yourself from harm, you don't have to put the
needs and wishes of others before your own.

Love Is Being Faithful in Prayer

Pray for your loved one and everyone who touches his or
her life. Also pray for wisdom for yourself in the situation
and for those who influence you regarding your loved one.
Paul prayed day and night for the people God put into his
life (2 Tim. 1:3).

However, prayer isn't all you're called to do. Some Christians use prayer as an excuse to avoid the responsibility to take action and make changes that need to be made. God wants you to put your faith into action (James 2:14). Jesus told us to love, do good, bless, *and* pray for those who mistreat us (Luke 6:27-31).

Love Is Bearing Good Fruit

"Live as children of light (for the fruit of the light consists in all goodness, righteousness and truth)" (Eph. 5:8-9). What is the fruit of your action or inaction in your dysfunctional relationship? Does it produce righteousness in your loved one and yourself? Or does it result in sin, dissension, anger, and other evils? Are you allowing your loved one to continue in destructive behaviors without consequences? Is what you're doing leaving you feeling discouraged, angry, bitter, ashamed, and broken? Are your actions exposing sin and bringing it to the light, or are you covering up sin in the hope of keeping the peace for the time being?

Taking a hard look at the fruit can help you determine if your choices are right. Before listing the fruit of the Spirit, Paul lists the acts of a sinful nature: "sexual immorality, impurity and debauchery; idolatry and witchcraft; hatred, discord, jealousy, fits of rage, selfish ambition, dissensions, factions and envy; drunkenness, orgies, and the like" (Gal. 5:19-21). He then lists the fruit of the Spirit: "love, joy, peace, patience, kindness, goodness, faithfulness, gentleness and self-control" (Gal. 5:22-23). Which of these lists best describes your difficult relationship? Passive tolerance of wrong results in sin in your life and your loved one's life by the fruit it produces: anger, resentment, self-pity, careless words, contentiousness, pride, unbelief, revenge, enabling, hatred, turmoil, and sinful acts. It destroys physical health, dignity, and self-esteem. It is also a bad example to others.

Eph. 5:11 says, "Have nothing to do with the fruitless

deeds of darkness, but rather expose them." This means you are not to cover up or make excuses for evil. Gal. 6:7-9 says, "Do not be deceived: God cannot be mocked. A man reaps what he sows. The one who sows to please his sinful nature, from that nature will reap destruction; the one who sows to please the Spirit, from the Spirit will reap eternal life. Let us not become weary in doing good, for at the proper time we will reap a harvest if we do not give up." When you interfere with God's law of reaping and sowing by preventing your loved one from reaping the fruit of his or her actions, you are acting out of fear and insecurity rather than out of trust and faith. How many times have you known what was right in your heart but not been willing to suffer or allow temporary negative consequences—so you did not take a stand? I ignored that conviction many times and deeply regretted it when I saw the fruit of ungodliness in my relationships.

Loving your difficult loved one means loving him or her enough to have strong boundaries that say no to sin in his or her life, in your life, and in your home. God does not leave us alone. He goes after us, convicts us, allows us to suffer consequences and pain, and disciplines us with the purpose of bringing us to repentance (Heb. 12:5-11).

Standing up for good means standing against sin even if it causes unpleasant consequences for you or your loved one. 1 Pet. 3:17 says, "It is better, if it is God's will, to suffer for doing good than for doing evil." When you take a stand against wrong, any consequences you endure qualify as suffering for doing good. Taking a stand against sin is often more difficult than passively allowing things to continue. You will suffer for not taking a stand as you endure mistreatment, anxiety, emotional turmoil, and other difficulties. It is better to suffer for doing good. That kind of suffering pleases God.

Love Is Asking for Respect

Respect is a necessary part of a good relationship, demonstrated by showing honor and esteem toward people you value. God told children to respect their parents (Lev. 19:3), the Israelites to respect the elderly (Lev. 19:32), slaves to respect their masters (Eph. 6:5), wives to respect their husbands (Eph. 5:33), husbands to respect their wives (1 Pet. 3:7), and the church to respect elders and pastors (1 Thess. 5:12).

The Prov. 31 woman "is clothed with strength and dignity" (v. 25), and "her husband is respected at the city gate" (v. 23). Strength is defined as either an intellectual or moral power as a result of influence and authority. Dignity is defined as conducting oneself in a way that indicates self-respect. You cannot demand that your difficult loved one treat you with respect, but you will get more respect when you treat him or her with respect and *expect* the same in return.

In Matt. 5:38-39 Jesus said, "You have heard that it was said, 'Eye for eye, and tooth for tooth.' But I tell you, do not resist an evil person. If someone strikes you on the right cheek, turn to him the other also." Jesus used this example to explain the differences between the old covenant and the new covenant. Old covenant law required an eye for an eye as punishment. Jesus was not condoning physical abuse or the tolerance of mistreatment but was encouraging an attitude of forgiveness rather than revenge. He was not saying you could not ask for respect in a relationship.

Love Is Maintaining Your Rights

Some mistakenly believe Christians do not have rights, proving their point by saying that we're to lay down our lives for others and die to self, thereby implying that it's wrong to ask for our needs to be met, to say no to abuse or mistreatment, or to demand respect.

As Christians, we do give up the right to having sin in our lives. Col. 3:3 says, "You died, and your life is now hidden with Christ in God." Verse 5 continues with "Put to death, therefore, whatever belongs to your earthly nature."

We are told to put our sinful natures to death. The death we experience is a death to self and to sin. We die to self when we forgive, respond with gentleness to anger, choose right over wrong, and stand up for right even though we're afraid. We die to self when we serve one another. Dying to self does not mean allowing others to mistreat us without standing up for what's right or not asking for our needs to be met in relationships.

Governments guarantee rights to their citizens. Paul reminded the Roman authorities twice that his rights as a Roman citizen were being violated (Acts 16:37; 22:25). America was founded on a belief that we have inalienable rights given by God. We do not consider it sin to demand our inalienable rights from the government. We defend ourselves to make sure we're treated fairly in civil and criminal matters. We have rights under the law: the right to property, due process, free speech, legal representation, free association, religious freedom, and to be considered innocent until proven guilty. If we have no rights as Christians, why don't we just lay down these rights any time we're challenged? Because we understand that in these areas it's not inconsistent with Scripture to make a stand for justice. Neither is it unloving to take a stand for rights in relationships.

Love Is Long-suffering and Persevering

"Love never fails" (1 Cor. 13:8). "Long-suffering" means enduring injury or trouble long and patiently. It means hanging in there through rough times rather than walking away from difficult relationships when you first encounter a problem. It means fighting for the relationship and for the good of the other person. It does not mean, however, accepting anything that comes your way without responding appropriately.

Love perseveres (1 Cor. 13:7). Persevering means persistently pursuing something even though you encounter opposition and obstacles. God's love motivates Him to allow consequences and to discipline us for our own good in order to produce righteousness in our lives.

Love holds out for the best outcome and does not stop even when a relationship is estranged. It means we continue behaving in a loving way even when the object of our love is rebellious, confused, and unloving. Like Jesus, the Good Shepherd, it continues to seek the lost sheep (Luke 15:4-7).

Love Is Gentle

Don't confuse gentleness with walking on eggshells to "keep the peace." Rom. 12:18 says, "If it is possible, as far as it depends on you, live at peace with everyone." This peace refers to harmonious, reconciled relationships, not the absence of conflict. We are to do everything we can to have good relationships with all the people in our lives. Being a doormat does not result in genuinely harmonious relationships.

Gentleness and quietness are associated with meekness and describe an inner spirit that rests and trusts in God regardless of outward circumstances. Isa. 30:15 says, "In quietness and confidence shall be your strength" (NKJV). It is the opposite of a spirit of unrest and turmoil.

This does not prevent you from speaking the truth or confronting wrong. When you refuse to speak out against what you know is wrong, your spirit is actually full of unrest, fear, anger, resentment, distrust, and confusion. Love is administered in a spirit of quiet strength and confidence in God.

Love Is Forgiving

Forgiveness is often misunderstood to be passive tolerance and acceptance of everything without boundaries. Your loved one may manipulatively say that you're required to forgive him or her because God tells you to. You do need to forgive, or you'll become resentful and bitter—but forgiveness does not mean that you lie down and say, "Step on me again—I like it," nor does it mean you passively accept everything your loved one does without limits and consequences. Forgiveness means only that you give up your right to take revenge.

Dysfunctional relationships are quite complicated. However, the biblical truths still apply. As we explore the remaining transforming principles, you'll be enabled to love your tough loved one with loving toughness.

REACH OUT

Two are better than one, because they have a good return for their work: If one falls down, his friend can help him up. But pity the man who falls and has no one to help him up! —Eccles. 4:9-10

Y ou may isolate yourself from other people by not being honest about your problems or by pulling away from family, friends, and outside interests for different reasons:

- You're embarrassed and don't want anyone to know the truth about your life.
- You're too overwhelmed to have energy for outside things.
- You think no one understands.
- You have talked to people and been hurt.
- You feel you're betraying your loved one if you talk about the problems.
- You believe Christians should not have emotional problems.

As long as you keep your problems to yourself, you'll stay stuck. God wants you to reach out when you're hurting. Christians have emotional problems just as they have physical problems. Christ bore your transgressions, weaknesses, problems, and sorrows on the Cross (Isa. 53:4-5). His plan is for you to be healed in the context of loving and honest relationships with others.

BREAKING OUT OF ISOLATION

It's important for you to realize that you're not alone. Many people have problems similar to yours. If you feel alone, it may be because you're not being open so that others can share their similar experiences. Admitting your problems, faults, and weaknesses to others is an important part of healing (James 5:13-16). Openness also benefits others, making it safe for them to be honest.

Mitch and Lori were in a Bible study with six other couples. They were struggling with their 24-year-old son's drug addiction and criminal behavior. They hadn't brought it up because everyone else seemed to be living such victorious Christian lives. Finally, they decided to share their pain, guilt, arguments, and doubt. To their surprise, other couples were going through difficulties too. The group grew closer as they shared their struggles and supported each other.

SUPPORT FROM FAMILY AND FRIENDS

Family members and close friends may not always be the best people to help you since they have an emotional connection to you and might not stay neutral in their responses. They may even be emotionally connected to your difficult loved one, or they may feel free to react impatiently, critically, and angrily with you.

Emotional reactivity is common in people closely related to one another. Each person responds out of his or her personal and emotional perspective, as well as his or her connection to you and your loved one. For instance, each family member and friend may react differently to your concern regarding your father's drinking. Your husband may not have patience out of fear of how it will affect your lives. Your mother and sister may be in denial, reacting angrily with you for bringing it up. Your brother may have severed his relationship with your father and thinks you are strange to be suffering so. Your best friend may have a healthy family and not understand your experience, thereby minimizing your concerns. Another friend may have had a previous problem with addiction and be very supportive. Talking to an outsider will allow you to get the point of view of someone who's not so close to the problem.

You can choose how many details you tell about your difficulties. Be selective. Don't tell intimate details that you may later regret. Balance your need to talk with the privacy needs of your loved one, especially with people who know him or her. It may not be a good idea to confide in his or her coworker, boss, or spouse. But always remember that talking about the problem is not betrayal. You can and should get whatever help you need to take care of yourself and deal appropriately with the situation.

CHURCH SUPPORT

We often go to church pretending everything is great. We worship together but don't share our pain. Some churches are better at merging relational, spiritual, and emotional issues, while other churches focus on the spiritual as if it's distinctly separate. Jesus spoke honestly and directly about whatever concerns people were experiencing at the moment. The apostle Paul did the same.

It's good to get advice from the spiritual leaders God has placed in your life, but remember that they're not trained counselors and may not have experience in what you're dealing with. You should respect them and cooperate with them to advance the gospel so that you don't make their work for the Lord more difficult (1 Thess. 5:12-13; Heb. 13:17). But you're not bound to do whatever they tell you to do. It's your responsibility to seek answers until you have sufficient information. "Plans fail for lack of counsel, but with many advisers they succeed" (Prov. 15:22).

Some Christians give pat answers to all of life's problems: "Pray about it." "Trust God." "All things work together for good." These responses are not unbiblical, but they don't *feel* supportive.

Maybe you fear being honest with other Christians because you feel ashamed. Maybe you're convinced that you don't even belong in church when you have so much turmoil in your heart and life. In reality, God calls the unrighteous, not the righteous (Matt. 9:13). The more difficult your life is, the more you need Him. Paul told the Thessalonians to "encourage one another and build each other up" (1 Thess. 5:11). It's God's plan that others strengthen and lift you up when you're low—but you have to let them.

SEEK PROFESSIONAL HELP

Counseling gives you helpful professional insight for your problems. "He who walks with the wise grows wise" (Prov. 13:20). A counselor also helps people work through problems together, acting as a mediator, which decreases resistance. At times it's helpful to go to counseling with your loved one; at other times it's best to go alone. If you ask and he or she refuses, go alone.

Counselors use different approaches, so it's important for you to find one who uses a style that works for you. Some focus heavily on your past and childhood as a key to help you understand yourself today. Others focus on finding practical solutions for your problem. Some counselors do more listening, while others give more direct input.

Going to a Christian counselor may help you feel more relaxed about the advice you're getting; however, it's not always possible if the counselor your insurance company will pay for isn't a Christian and you can't afford to pay for it yourself. Non-Christian counselors have knowledge and insights that will help you. However, no matter whom you go to, you have to reconcile what's said with your faith. It's up to you to use discernment and discard what's not scriptural.

If you've tried counseling and it hasn't been successful, it may be that you were with the wrong counselor or you may not have been ready to hear what the counselor told you. No matter what your past experience has been, don't give up on counseling as an option for getting help.

Finding a good counselor may take some work. Ask people you know if they can recommend a good one. See if counseling is provided by your medical insurance or church. Most counselors have a sliding-fee scale based on income. Never be afraid to change to another counselor if the one you are seeing isn't helping you.

SUPPORT GROUPS

Support groups consist of people who share a common, unifying experience or issue. Taking part in a support group is a significant step in learning to value yourself enough to begin building a better life. The first thing you will learn is that you're not alone. When you're isolated, you feel that you're the only one with problems; from that viewpoint it's hard to see your way out of the situation. It will be an important step just to learn that other people have similar feelings and problems.

You'll gain hope by meeting others whose lives have improved, and you'll get ideas for handling your own dilemmas. You'll understand yourself better as you hear others share their feelings and struggles. You'll have people to call when you need help between meetings. No one tells you what decisions to make or exactly what to do; they simply share their experiences.

God wants us to comfort others with the comfort we have received in similar trials (1 Cor. 1:4). Those who have experienced similar circumstances can be the most empathetic and helpful. It's not an instant cure, but the beginning of a life-changing process.

Many people join support groups expecting to learn how to force their loved ones to change and find out they can change only themselves. But then as *they* begin to change, their relationships begin to improve.

There are many support groups for people in dysfunctional relationships. They include "twelve step" groups like

Al-Anon, Codependents Anonymous, Adult Children of Alcoholics, Codependents of Sex Addicts, Gam-Anon, Nar-
Anon Family Groups, and Tough Love. Some Christians feel
uncomfortable with the group's referring to God as simply a
"higher power." This has resulted in churches starting their
own programs and support groups with the acknowledgment that their higher power is Jesus Christ. Overcomers
Outreach and Celebrate Recovery are the largest, with
meetings around the country and internationally.

All of these groups are based on anonymity and confi-
dentiality, meaning that your attendance and what you say
are not disclosed to outsiders, giving everyone freedom to
share openly. If you don't know of any groups, call larger
churches, look in your phonebook, or check the Internet.

Some churches and pastors say that all you need is salvation. Their assumption is that relationships will be restored
when you become a new creation (2 Cor. 5:17). In reality,
getting saved does not instantly remove problems. In fact, it
can sometimes make you more aware of doing right—creat-
ing new dilemmas. It's not wrong to go to medical doctors
for physical health problems; it's also not wrong to go to
support groups or counselors for help with emotional, spiritual, and relational problems. The steps are based on scriptural principles. God uses all types of things to help you
heal and grow.

Support groups vary based on the type of group and the
setting. Go to several meetings, and if you feel uncomfortable, try something else. Each group and meeting will feel
different, depending on the people attending and the focus. Large meetings give you less opportunity to share but a
chance to hear many different people. Small groups allow
you to do more personal sharing, are less threatening, and
allow you to form closer bonds.

Support groups encourage members to find a sponsor or

mentor to help with personal problems. This person is someone who has gone through similar difficulties and has effectively applied the steps to his or her life. You're encouraged to call between meetings to discuss specific problems.

A note of warning: Don't stop going to whatever support group you find when your life starts improving slightly. It takes hard work to make lasting changes. The truth is that difficult problems, like the ones you have, don't go away quickly. The problems resurface after a short time when they're not properly and adequately resolved.

Your family and friends may not understand your need to get support from a group, especially if they don't want to admit the problems. If you feel you would benefit from a support group, go anyway. Without change, your life will not improve. If your family is not able to support your best interest, you must. You don't need anyone's approval or permission to take care of yourself.

You may feel as if you're betraying your loved one when you break out of your isolation. You may feel being faithful and loyal means not talking about your problems. As long as your motive is pure, meaning you're not seeking to discredit or destroy him or her out of anger or revenge, and you're doing it because it's good for you or your loved one, it's not betrayal. Telling your best friend, your family, your pastor, or going to a support group is not a betrayal. Staying quiet to appease or cover up for him or her is not a good reason to keep silent. In fact, it's often the secrecy that surrounds the dysfunction that allows it to continue. One of the common rules in a dysfunctional family is that it's not OK to talk about problems. You can minimize the defensiveness by stating that you're getting help for yourself.

Unhealthy and Healthy Relationship Differences

All relationships have problems at one time or the other,

but people in healthy relationships discuss problems, respect each other's differences, and come to a mutual understanding and resolution. Both parties respect the other's freedom of choice, individuality, and personal boundaries. Both parties are able to handle their own emotions, empathize with each other, engage in self-examination, admit when they're wrong, correct faulty thinking, consider other viewpoints, and make necessary adjustments. Intimacy is the result of honesty and vulnerability. Healthy people look inward to evaluate their thoughts, attitudes, feelings, and behaviors. They're secure enough to express the truth about themselves, including their strengths and weaknesses, and accept others' truths, remaining unthreatened by others' opinions, emotions, and differences.

Unhealthy people are not able to do those things. They're disconnected from what's going on emotionally, relationally, mentally, and spiritually within themselves and others. They're insecure, threatened by others' emotions, reacting by controlling or fixing. They don't have the skills to communicate directly, empathize, self-analyze, and admit faults. This results in misunderstandings, unresolved issues, emotional pain, frustration, distancing, disappointment, and disillusionment.

Healthy relationships require two individuals who are independent adults with the ability to love and receive love, respect and accept each other, resolve conflict, communicate directly, be honest, be vulnerable, be emotionally supportive, cooperate, trust, and take responsibility for themselves and their choices.

Difficult relationships result when at least one of the individual's personal problems interferes with his or her ability to love and receive love, communicate directly and honestly, and cooperate. Instead, there's competition, unresolved conflict, hostility and anger, disrespect, distrust, irresponsibility, blame, lack of acceptance, and struggle for control.

In unhealthy relationships, arguments frequently follow the same pattern regardless of the actual issue: denying, attacking, defending, avoiding, deflecting, and accusing—all designed to prevent dealing with the issue. Trent tried to talk to his wife about her drinking. Every time he brought it up, she got angry with him for criticizing her. They argued about his tone of voice, lack of support toward her, and long hours at the office. Somehow she never addressed her drinking problem. They both walked away feeling angry, unloved, and distanced. The issue was, as usual, unresolved.

DYSFUNCTIONAL AND FUNCTIONAL FAMILY DIFFERENCES

In a healthy family, each member's individual needs and differences are respected and valued. There's free expression of opinions and feelings. The family shares responsibilities and offers support. There's unconditional love and approval. Discipline, rules, and boundaries are consistent. Conflict is resolved. Forgiveness is offered and received. There's spontaneity, fun, and laughter. It's safe to trust. A family may not have all these characteristics all the time, but the more they have, the healthier they are, and the greater the self-worth and satisfaction of all family members.

Dysfunctional families are composed of unhealthy people and relationships. "Dysfunctional" means not functioning or broken. A family is more than the individuals—it's a system governed by rules that determine what behavior is acceptable and unacceptable. When someone in a dysfunctional family breaks a rule, he or she is punished in some way: by disapproval, withdrawal, anger, ridicule, isolation, shame, or punishment. The problem is that the rules are also dysfunctional. There are five common rules in a dysfunctional family: Don't talk. Don't feel. Don't trust. Don't be selfish. Don't make mistakes.

"Don't talk" means that problems are denied and not

discussed in or outside the home. Talking about "the problem" upsets the status quo. Instead, everyone pretends that things are OK, keeping the family secret.

"Don't feel" means no one admits his or her feelings. If the person does, feelings are discounted, excused, punished, or interpreted as disrespectful or betrayal.

"Don't trust" comes from the inconsistency each feels from contradictory and confusing double messages, broken promises, conflicting words and actions, and lies. Should one trust what was said or what is seen and felt? Some examples of double messages are "Always tell the truth; pretend, because I don't want to know the truth." "I love you; I don't like you." "I want you near me; leave me alone." "I'll do it—I promise; I'll do it next time."

"Don't be selfish" comes from the inability of the family to allow all individuals to get their needs met and be themselves. Any family member who dares to put his or her needs first expresses disloyalty to the family system and is considered selfish. However, typically there is one member who expects everyone to cater to his or her needs. This is often the addict, the controller, or the angry one.

"Don't make mistakes" comes from the inability of the family to deal with problems. There's little tolerance or patience for error. Forgiveness is not freely given. Criticism and resentment abound. There's no grace. Conditional love replaces the security of unconditional love.

Children find ways to cope with the unpredictability, instability, and painful emotions to bring order and balance to their lives as much as possible. One way they do this is by adopting roles in the family. Some children become overly responsible, taking care of their parents, siblings, and the household. Some become super-good, attempting to be loved for their achievements. Others become invisible so they don't add more demands to the overwhelmed family system. Some develop problems in an attempt to get the family to look at the truth or to take the focus off the real issues, allowing the parents the opportunity to unite to deal with the child's difficulty. Children also take on the role of the peacemaker, attempting to resolve disputes. These roles are often carried into adulthood. Are you still filling your childhood role?

Children from dysfunctional families grow up to be adult children of dysfunctional families lacking communication and conflict resolution skills, positive self-esteem, and healthy boundaries. Exod. 20:5 describes a generational curse in which the sins of the fathers are passed on to the third and fourth generations. Adults repeat the mistakes and relationship behaviors of their parents by marrying someone with similar problems and reacting to their own children the same way their parents treated them. You may have come from a dysfunctional family and be repeating the mistakes of your parents. They may have repeated the mistakes of their parents (your grandparents). It's never too late to make changes to break this generational repetition.

COMMON RELATIONSHIP DIFFICULTIES

Many things contribute to a dysfunctional relationship. In Prov. 2, Solomon recommends searching for wisdom and understanding, as knowledge and discretion will protect and save from wicked people and their perverse words. Gaining an understanding of the problems you and your loved ones are encountering will enable you to use wisdom to guide your actions.

Information is available through books, support groups, the Internet, counselors, and others. If you're not sure what you're dealing with, talk to a counselor to put a label on the problem.

General Dysfunction

Many relationships are difficult because one or more of the individuals involved in them exhibit unhealthy traits such as being manipulative, controlling, insecure, dependent, noncommunicative, self-centered, nonintrospective, irresponsible, uncooperative, immature, angry, nonempathetic, self-pitying, rigid, and vengeful. Many of these traits come from replaying the dynamics and unresolved hurts of past relationships in ways that disrupt current relationships.

Irresponsibility is a common cause of a difficult relationship. If your loved one is not responsible in his or her choices, you may feel it's your responsibility to pick up the pieces by paying the bills, taking care of undone tasks, and attempting to direct and control to prevent the irresponsibility. You may bail him or her out because you feel you have no other choice and yet resent it at the same time.

You may disagree with the choices your loved one is making and the way he or she is living, feeling that it's your responsibility to make him or her choose differently.

Mental Disorders

A mental disorder is characterized by behavior or psychological symptoms that result in distress and impairment in one or more areas of life. Many types of mental illnesses exist. Some of the more common ones are mood disorders, schizophrenia, anxiety disorders, eating disorders, dementia, and personality disorders. Many of the mental disorders improve with proper medications and treatment.

A mood is an emotional state that affects the way a person views life. Depression is the most common mood disorder and is sometimes caused by neurotransmitter imbalances. Depression is manifested by a change in functioning, a depressed or sad mood, hopelessness, irritability, decreased interest in normal activities, weight gain or loss, sleep problems, tiredness or loss of energy, decreased sense of self-worth, inability to concentrate, and sometimes thoughts of suicide. Depression ranges from mild to severe. Some people are chronically depressed; you may never have known them to be any other way. Others suffer depressive episodes in which a definite change is noticed.

It can be difficult to deal with a depressed person who lacks motivation to improve. Depressed people often hook you with self-pity, victimization, and martyrdom to get you to feel sorry for them and take care of them. You may even notice *yourself* feeling depressed by their pervasive negativity.

Bipolar disorder is a mood disorder manifested by periods of mania with increased self-esteem, energy, and activity; decreased sleep; poor judgment; irritability; and racing thoughts. The mania can range from mild to severe. The main noticeable symptom is the change in moods and the extreme nature of the changes. Drug or alcohol abuse is often used to mask the highs and lows to create a more normal state. In extreme cases the person can become psychotic and lose touch with reality.

Bipolar disorder can be treated with psychotropic medications. However, it's not unusual for people with this disorder to stop taking their medication when they feel better, which means that they'll go through more mood swings.

Schizophrenics lose touch with reality. Their behavior and speech may be bizarre and disorganized. They may have hallucinations (false sensations) or delusions (false beliefs). They may have reduced speech, emotions, activity, and movement or exaggerated and unusual movements. Medication is usually helpful.

Anxiety disorders take many forms. The anxiety may be manifested in extreme and persistent worrying about multiple things. Post-traumatic stress disorder results from exposure to a life-threatening event that's re-experienced mentally and emotionally or avoided by a refusal to think or talk about the event. Panic attacks involve a sudden onset of fear or anxiety with physiological symptoms such as difficulty breathing, rapid heartbeat, dizziness, or a feeling of losing control. Phobias involve fears of specific objects or situations. Agoraphobia involves a fear of being in a place where escape is difficult or help may be unavailable in the event of a panic attack. Anxiety can also be manifested by repetitive obsessive and compulsive actions.

Eating disorders include anorexia and bulimia. Bulimics binge-eat, consuming abnormally large amounts of food in a short time with subsequent measures to prevent weight gain, such as purgatives (laxatives and vomiting), excessive exercise, or fasting. Anorexia is an intense fear of gaining weight, resulting in a refusal to eat or frequent purging after eating. It's associated with a distorted body image in which the anorexic perceives the body as fat even though it's underweight. Both disorders can eventually cause significant physical damage.

Dementia is characterized by a neurological impairment that affects memory, language skills, and the ability to reason and function in daily routines. It's more common in the elderly. Alzheimer's is a type of dementia.

Personality disorders are lifelong patterns of behavior that affect emotions, thoughts, perceptions, and relationships. Common ones include anti-social personality disorder, narcissistic personality disorder, dependent personality disorder, and borderline personality disorder.

Antisocial personality disorder is a longstanding pattern of aggression, impulsivity, breaking of rules, disregard for others' property and safety, lying, stealing, irresponsibility, and breaking of laws and rules without feeling guilt. The reckless and defiant behavior often starts in childhood, when it's diagnosed as conduct disorder.

Narcissism is a form of self-centeredness that's common in addicts, controllers, and abusers. However, a severe form is diagnosed as narcissistic personality disorder and is characterized by an exaggerated self-image, a feeling of being unique, expectations of special treatment, a need to be admired, a tendency to use people, an inability to be empathetic, and an arrogant attitude. When you're around a narcissist, you'll feel as if you don't exist. Narcissistic parents have difficulty seeing the needs of their children since they're so self-absorbed and typically blame others for their inadequacies.

Dependent personality disorder is caused by an extreme need to be taken care of, manifested by clingy and dependent behavior. It's associated with difficulty making decisions, taking responsibility, and expressing disagreement, plus a fear of being alone.

Borderline personality disorder is a persistent pattern of difficult and unstable relationships, poor self-image, fear of abandonment, extreme and damaging impulsivity, self-destructive acts, mood instability, inappropriate anger, and possibly paranoia or loss of identity. Borderlines struggle with feeling overly attached or abandoned in relationships, thereby fluctuating between positive and hostile emotions toward others.

Self-mutilation or "cutting" is an increasingly common problem. When cutters feel intense psychological pain, they hurt themselves physically to either escape or express the pain. They frequently have difficulty handling or verbally expressing their emotions. Family members often react with fear and denial or by discouraging the cutting. Facing the cutting by openly talking about it and getting help are better options. Many cutters are victims of child abuse and neglect. They often have additional diagnoses of eating disorders, bipolar disorder, depression, or borderline personality disorder.

It's not your job to diagnose a mental illness. A qualified counselor, psychiatrist, or medical doctor has to make the diagnosis. It's enough for you to recognize that the problems in your loved one's life are serious enough to warrant outside help.

Mental illness is something the person has no choice in having; however, you're still justified and obligated to do what it takes to protect yourself and maintain a decent quality of life and expect your loved one to do what he or she can to get help. You can do what's appropriate in terms of protective and caring interventions for yourself and your loved ones.

Addictions

An addict is someone who is dependent on using a mind-altering substance or activity in order to cope. It could be alcohol, drugs, gambling, sex, pornography, work, or anything used repeatedly to escape feelings and problems. King Solomon advised avoiding anything in excess: "Listen, my son, and be wise, and keep your heart on the right path. Do not join those who drink too much wine or gorge themselves on meat, for drunkards and gluttons become poor, and drowsiness clothes them in rags" (Prov. 23:19-21).

Addicts are often self-centered, unable to empathize, emotionally immature, unreliable, resentful, dishonest, unreasonable, and blaming. These characteristics are often present even if they're not using their drug of choice and are called the "dry drunk syndrome."

Addictions worsen over time as the frequency increases and the problems escalate in all areas: work, relationships, social, financial, physical, and personal.

Until addicts are ready to face their addictions, they will adamantly deny reality, blaming problems on someone else, most often their families. They may promise to stop, but the obsession is strong—so they do it again, even if they don't want to. "As a dog returns to its vomit, so a fool repeats his folly" (Prov. 26:11). In order to change, addicts have to get to the point at which they admit they have a problem and will do whatever it takes to stop. That usually takes "hitting bottom," where the price they pay for the addiction becomes significant enough to them to compel them to change. An absence of the addictive substance usually causes psychological and/or physical withdrawal, making cessation difficult.

Watch your expectations when the addict promises change. Relapse is common. In addition, sobriety brings a whole new set of problems as the addict must now face life without "the crutch" and the family has to adjust to a new person interacting with them on differing terms.

Drug and Alcohol Addictions

A drug addict or alcoholic is someone who can't stop drinking or using drugs. He or she does not have to drink or use drugs every day to be addicted. In fact, many are periodic users, partaking only on weekends or periodically for days at a time. They can be successful in business and do fairly well at holding their lives together, at least for a while, but the addiction eventually affects one or more areas of their lives negatively. Substances can also be abused without being dependent on them.

Sexual Addictions

Sexual addiction refers to an excessive and obsessive focus on sex. It can involve pornography, frequent masturbation, phone sex, Internet chat rooms, prostitution, or many affairs. The sex addict usually withdraws, acts out, and then is filled with shame and fear over the behavior. The cycle repeats itself again. Sex is a very powerful stimulant that leaves lasting mental images and associations in the brain. The sex addict becomes hooked to the chemical stimulation associated with the stimulus. Sex addicts tend to be emotionally withdrawn in relationships and have difficulty with intimacy.

Gambling

Gambling is classified as an addiction due to the loss of control and the addictive nature of the behavior. The typical lying, denial, anger, blame, and unpredictability that come with other addictions accompany it. The gambler has difficulty stopping, even when broke. Many lose everything they own. As Solomon said, "He who works his land will have abundant food, but he who chases fantasies lacks judgment" (Prov. 12:11).

Workaholism and Other Excesses

Anything that's done in excess can be damaging to relationships. Activities can be used to compensate for internal and external weaknesses, feelings, and unmet needs or to avoid dealing with uncomfortable emotional and relationship issues. The resultant lack of intimacy is frustrating for the family, who feels disillusioned, angry, resentful, and ignored. It can be anything: work, sports, friends, volunteering, hobbies, television, the Internet, or a single relationship with one person to the exclusion of another.

Abuse

Physical, emotional, and verbal abuse is demeaning and destructive. Prov. 14:17 says, "A quick-tempered man does foolish things, and a crafty man is hated." Abusive people see relationships as power struggles. As a result, when they feel powerless and insecure, they react by trying to control and manipulate others through punishment and fear. The abused often feel fear, confusion, and hurt; attempt to please the abuser; and suffer from low self-esteem. Most children from dysfunctional homes have suffered some form of abuse.

Anger

Anger is destructive when in excess or acted out in sinful ways. Hostile and excessive anger is damaging. Prov. 27:4 says, "Anger is cruel and fury overwhelming." It is difficult to feel safe and valued when someone is continually angry with you.

Passive aggressive anger is subtle but equally damaging. The passive aggressive person does not admit anger, mistakes conflict and criticism as an attack, and is defensive. Anger underlies purposeful actions like being late, refusing to cooperate, forgetting, and making mistakes. Introspection is lacking, and resentments run high. It can be difficult to recognize but extremely frustrating to deal with.

Physical Problems

Chronic or permanent physical illness causes stress and imbalance in a relationship, making it difficult to draw lines regarding responsibilities and emotional reactions. Adults with learning disabilities or attention deficit disorder may have difficulty following through with tasks, listening, being responsible, and controlling their impulses and emotions.

Sudden changes in personality can be related to underlying physical illnesses. In these cases, it's important to encourage your loved one to get a medical checkup.

THE ROLLER COASTER

Adding to the confusion, dysfunctional relationships often experience ups and downs that occur without warning. Things may appear to be getting better and then make a quick turn for the worse. This adds to the frustration, confusion, and hurt. You may wonder which person your loved one really is: the good or the bad. The answer is both. Even the most difficult person has good moments and positive character traits.

Not knowing when things will blow up next keeps you in a constant state of insecurity and nervousness as you find yourself spending a great deal of time and energy trying to anticipate the next event. It's important to understand the problem the best you can, but ultimately your focus needs to be on changing yourself.

CHANGE YOURSELF, NOT YOUR LOVED ONE

Each one should test his own actions. Then he can take pride in himself, without comparing himself to somebody else, for each one should carry his own load. —Gal. 6:4-5

You may believe that in order for your life to improve, your difficult loved one has to change first. You may also believe that you're responsible for making him or her change. Chances are that you spend a tremendous amount of energy thinking about what he or she is doing or not doing. You try not to worry and obsess, but you just can't help it. You attempt to manipulate his or her choices so that he or she will do the right things: go to work, stop drinking or drugging, treat you right, act responsibly, make wise choices, understand your feelings and concerns, follow through on promises, or respect your boundaries. You may try to force change by nagging, pleading, threatening, screaming, covering up for mistakes, taking over responsibilities, cutting off the relationship, talking to others about the situation, trying to get others involved, overlooking wrongs, giving in, sacrificing, placating, keeping quiet, or talking too much.

You may even believe that *you're* at fault—at least partially. You may believe that you've caused his or her behavior. Maybe you've tried to change yourself—expecting reciprocal change. If you feel responsible (perhaps your loved one has tried to make you feel responsible), you may be trying to make amends by doing things to make up for your mistakes in hopes of minimizing your guilt. Maybe you try to be accepting, loving, and forgiving. You may always be there to pick up the pieces, overlooking your own needs and feelings. Finally, you get angry and react in ways that leave you feeling torn and unhappy with yourself.

You've done everything you can think of, but the problem still exists and you have no peace. Your attempts to force change have left you feeling empty, angry, resentful, and worn out. You may even be angry with God for not answering your prayers.

Eventually your life is dominated by your loved one's behavior. All your other relationships—work, finances, and physical and spiritual well-being—are affected. When you believe others need to change first—either on their own or miraculously with God's intervention—you're neglecting the only area you truly *can* change: your own life.

EACH WILL GIVE AN ACCOUNT

Paul writes in 2 Cor. 5:10, "We must all appear before the judgment seat of Christ, that each one may receive what is due him for the things done while in the body, whether good or bad." You will stand before the Lord one day and give an account of your life, but you will not be required to account for anyone else's actions. You will answer only for what *you* did or did not do.

For years I tried to make people in my life make different choices, as if I my life depended on their changing. I spent so much energy trying to make them change that I mistreated them and others in the process. I became impatient, pushy, and judgmental, thinking I knew what was right for them. I did not. No one else can make the right choices for others. Only God truly knows what's best and what He requires of them. In fact, God will not judge people according to what we think they should do. He will judge them according to His standards: by what they have been given and the motives of their hearts (Luke 12:48).

When you give an account, God will want to know what you did as a steward of all He has given you—including spoken words and relationships (Matt. 12:36; 25:14-30). You will not be asked to explain others' choices, nor will you be able to use them as your excuse—so start focusing on changing your own actions.

How Do You Change Yourself?

Jesus said in Matt. 7:3-5 that we need to deal with our own faults and sins before we point to faults in others. Knowing our tendency to be less tolerant of faults in others than ourselves, He reminded us that we could be pointing to a "speck" in someone else's eye, all the while having a "plank" in our own. Calling us hypocrites, He warned us, "First take the plank out of your own eye, and then you will see clearly to remove the speck from your brother's eye."

Once you focus on changing yourself, you'll be able to view your loved one's choices differently. You'll be able to accept those choices without feeling the compulsion to force him or her to choose differently—even when his or her choices are wrong and cause pain to you and others you care about.

Give Up Being a Victim or a Martyr

As an adult, you should not allow yourself to be a victim. Believing you're trapped and helpless can make you *feel* like a victim. But you have options, and recognizing that you have choices helps to change your attitude toward your circumstances.

A martyr willingly suffers and sacrifices. A martyr says, "I have to take care of my adult son. What else is a good mother to do?" or "I know my family mistreats me, but that's OK—I'm used to it."

Martyrs want pity for their suffering and applause for their sacrifice. They suffer because they're unwilling to take responsibility for their own choices. Sacrifice is not wrong, but martyrdom is unhealthy when done for the wrong motives.

Prov. 21:29 says, "A wicked man puts up a bold front, but an upright man gives thought to his ways." Letting go of being a victim and a martyr allows you to give thought to your ways, recognize that you have options, and take full responsibility for your choices, moving you to the point of being in control of your own life.

Let Go of the Obsession

An obsession occurs when a person's thoughts or feelings are controlled by a persistent idea, desire, concern, or person. An obsessed person focuses on one thing to the exclusion of everything else and has difficulty functioning in other areas of his or her life. An obsessed person may be so consumed with what his or her loved one is doing that he or she may be unable to enjoy a vacation, a nice day, another relationship, or life. It becomes an all-consuming struggle, "for a man is a slave to whatever has mastered him" (2 Pet. 2:19).

June's obsession with her sister's eating disorder and cutting consumed her every thought. How could June make her see she needed help? The problem was that June had three children and a husband with whom she was frequently angry and impatient. They felt neglected by her. When her husband confronted her, her response was "How can I think about anyone else when she's having so much trouble?" Yes, obsession is all-encompassing.

Letting go of an obsession does not come naturally or easily. Yet God wants you to control your thoughts, not to be controlled or mastered by them (1 Cor. 6:12). He wants you to be able to control your responses to your thoughts and emotions. How can you be obedient to God when you're enslaved by another person, and your emotions and thoughts are ruled by his or her actions?

First, examine your obsession. How often are you thinking about the person or situation? What are you neglecting as a result of your obsession? Are you trying to control the situation by worrying? Are you trying to figure out how to fix the other person? Is guilt or fear the cause of your obsession? When you become aware of the reasons behind your obsession, it will be easier to control.

Counter the obsession. If it's fear, counter it with a verse that reminds you to trust God. If it's control, remind yourself that you can't control someone else. If it's guilt, remind yourself that you're not responsible for someone else's choices.

Stop doing things that hook you, like checking up on your difficult person, asking questions, or wondering what he or she is doing and thinking. Stop doing anything that triggers your obsession.

Control your thoughts by forcing yourself to think about other things. God tells you to choose what you think about (Phil. 4:8-9). With divine power at your disposal, you're capable of taking every thought captive "to make it obedient to Christ" (2 Cor. 10:5). But it doesn't come without conscious effort and a battle. The good news is that it can be successfully done.

Admit That You're Powerless

Why do you obsess? The real cause of your obsession is a need to control situations and people. You want things your way because you believe that will make everything OK. Obsessing fools you into thinking that you're doing something about the situation.

Patty knew that if her sister Jane, who was diagnosed with bipolar disorder, would only take her medication, she would function fairly well—only she didn't. She tried to make her sister see the right doctors, take her medication, and stop harmful behavior during her mood swings. She often found herself thinking about the things she had to do to keep her sister from getting into trouble. Patty put so much energy into her sister that she ignored her husband, children, career, friends, and her own relationship with God. And in spite of everything she did, it wasn't working.

You've probably tried to force your loved one to change by keeping the peace, crying, begging, manipulation, threats, taking over responsibilities, and so on. But nothing really works.

The problem is that there's nothing you can do to force your loved one to change, and all your attempts keep you from improving your own life. In fact, your efforts may actually make the situation worse and even prevent change.

The remedy: Admit that you're powerless to accomplish what you want. You're 100 percent powerless concerning your loved one's choices. God created each of us with free will. He does not force us to do anything, even when He knows it's in our best interest. If God doesn't force His creation to change by using His power to control us, why do you think you can force your loved one to change?

Trying to control your loved one can be overt: nagging, arguing, lecturing, or getting angry. It can also be covert: keeping the peace by placating and pretending everything's OK, arranging things to prevent upsets, and using coercion. When you covertly or overtly control, you assume you know what's best for others. Only God knows what's in a person's heart and what it will take to soften and change it. Although God will not force people to change, He'll work in their lives in the way He knows is best. When you admit you're powerless, you're stepping aside and letting God take over.

Understand Yourself

In order to understand the difficulties in your dysfunctional relationship, you must understand yourself.

Everything that happens to you is processed through your own filter of preconceived ideas, assumptions, values, beliefs, and past experiences. All of these affect how you interpret and react to circumstances and people.

Every relationship and experience you've been a part of has changed you in some way. These experiences affect the way you react to people and the way you deal with problems. If as a child you couldn't trust your parents, you'll have difficulty trusting as an adult. If you didn't feel loved, you may need more attention. If one of your children took drugs, you'll be more watchful with your other children. Abused children tolerate abuse as adults. If your previous spouse had an affair, you'll be more distrustful of your current spouse.

Your personality also affects how you deal with things. Some people are naturally easy-going and adaptable, while others are controlling and critical. Some are naturally happy, while others are melancholy. It helps to understand your own natural strengths and weaknesses as well as to understand others' strengths and weaknesses. You can be more tolerant and compassionate when you accept that there are innate differences in the way people deal with things.

It's crucial that you learn to understand how your prior relationships, experiences, preconceptions, and personality affect the way you interpret what happens today.

No matter what your loved one's problems are, you're responsible for your own actions and reactions. He or she may drink, use drugs, neglect responsibilities, refuse to deal with the truth, abandon religion, mistreat you and others, but you choose the way *you* respond.

Your weaknesses contribute to relationship problems. You may be too dependent or too independent out of a fear of being vulnerable. You may have low self-esteem and be willing to tolerate mistreatment because you don't feel worthy of being treated better. You may even believe it's the Christian thing to do. You may not know what you want and be afraid to make decisions, so you gravitate toward control-

ling people. Or you may need to be in control to feel secure, so you gravitate toward people you can dominate and
fix. You may not know who you are or what you want, so you
keep yourself busy taking care of other people. You may be
afraid to face a painful past, so you deny that you're affected
by it so you don't have to feel, think, or process the hurt.

Think about your childhood. Talk to your parents and
siblings about your home. Analyze your role in the family.
Did you feel responsible for your parents or siblings? Was
there an addiction or dysfunction in your family? Were you
sexually, verbally, emotionally, or physically abused? Were
your parents overly critical? Your goal is to come to a place
of understanding about the type of family you grew up in,
what your role in that family was, and how that affects who
you are today.

Second, look at your prior and current relationships. Are
there patterns? Are you passive and afraid to be yourself?
Are you treated with respect? Do you tend to feel insecure
and unloved? Do you tend to be controlling or controlled?
Do you take on too much responsibility or too little? Do you
have difficulty trusting? Are you an independent, healthy
adult with your own thoughts, goals, and interests, or are
you dependent on others to make a life for you? Do you
take responsibility for your actions, or do you blame others?
Are you aware of your feelings?

Understanding yourself will help you break the destructive patterns you repeat so you can maximize and enjoy
your strengths.

Feel Your Emotions

People in difficult relationships feel many intense emotions: fear, frustration, anxiety, hopelessness, sadness, regret, guilt, hurt, pain, despair, disappointment, love, hate,
shame. Those emotions are uncomfortable, but they must
be dealt with. God created you to feel. Feelings show you

what's in your heart and how things affect you. They're warning signs intended to guide you. There are also positive feelings like joy, happiness, satisfaction, and contentment. When you don't allow yourself to feel the painful ones, you prevent yourself from feeling the positive ones.

It's critical to your emotional, spiritual, and physical health that you pay attention to your feelings. In order to change your behavior, you must identify and accept those feelings and then decide what you want to do with them.

You can choose how you respond to feelings by controlling what you think about them. If you feel fearful, you can talk yourself through the fear by reminding yourself to trust God. When you feel irritated or angry, you can react and blame others or deal with the cause of your anger productively. Solomon warns against being "quickly provoked in your spirit" (Eccles. 7:9).

Difficult relationships make self-control hard as you continually deal with many complex issues and emotions. Thankfully, Paul states in Rom. 8:1 that there's no condemnation in Christ, because you have been set free from the law of sin. When you fail, God is ready to forgive and to help you to continue to strive toward the goal.

Own Your Feelings

Once you become aware of your feelings, be willing to own them instead of blaming circumstances or others for the way you feel. I'm sure many times you've heard someone say something like "You make me angry" or "You make me feel guilty." Actually, no one *makes* anyone feel anything. How you feel at any moment is affected by who you are: your past, your expectations, your present condition, your personality, and the meaning you attach to the experience.

You react differently to other people depending on your personality. Some people are naturally patient and meek. Others are assertive. This personality "filter" predisposes you to react a certain way. Owning your own emotions involves accepting responsibility for your unique feelings, perceptions, and reactions.

When you communicate, it's important to own your feelings and reactions by speaking in "I" statements. Your goal is to focus on how things affect you and your feelings rather than blaming others, forcing them to change, or insisting they see things your way. "You" statements blame others for your interpretation of their actions, placing the responsibility on them for your feelings. "I" statements own the reaction. Here are some examples of "I" statements versus "you" statements:

BLAMING	OWNING
You ignored me all night.	I felt neglected. I needed attention.
You drink too much.	I'm uncomfortable with your drinking.
If you cared about me, you would call.	I need to hear from you.
You were selfish to tell me no.	It was hard for me to accept your answer.
You don't love me.	I don't feel loved by you.
You were wrong.	I disagreed with your decision.
You're ruining your life.	I'm afraid of what might happen to you.

Weigh your answers rather than blurting out emotional accusations (Prov. 15:28). Take responsibility for your feelings and thoughts. You'll get a better response when you think before speaking.

Deal with Your Sin

Even when your difficult loved one is clearly in the wrong, your reactions and responses can make the problem worse. No matter what others do, you're responsible for your own response. Difficult relationships are just that: difficult. Others are doing things that really bother you—things that are wrong and destructive. You are in all likelihood correct that they're doing damaging things, but that does not excuse bad behavior on your part.

Kathy's adult daughter, Carrie, was taking drugs and was bulimic. Every time Kathy saw her, she nagged her about all the things she was doing wrong. Kathy and Carrie grew farther apart. Carrie's actions were hurting their relationship, but so was Kathy's nagging and anger. Kathy finally realized that she didn't trust Carrie but that Carrie could not trust her either, as she could not rely on her mom to treat her respectfully as an adult without judging and condemning her. After realizing she could not change her daughter but that she could change herself, Kathy apologized and changed her actions. Their relationship changed; they even enjoyed being together. Carrie eventually admitted that she had an eating disorder.

Prov. 15:1 says, "A gentle answer turns away wrath, but a harsh word stirs up anger." The Bible is full of verses that place the responsibility for your reactions on you. You are responsible for your part of the relationship. No matter how wrong someone else is, you must pay attention to your part. You may see your loved one not taking care of his or her responsibilities, but when you take over those responsibilities, you're choosing to do so and cannot blame that choice on your loved one. He or she may be hurting you, but you're not supposed to respond with revenge. He or she may be stubborn, arrogant, proud, or angry, but you don't have to be.

When you admit your wrongs, don't expect your loved one to admit his or her wrongs. It's nice when it happens, but it can't be a condition for your holding yourself accountable.

Check Your Motives

Changing yourself will require you to check your inner

motives. Jesus was concerned with motives throughout the Sermon on the Mount in Matt. 5—7. He continually contrasted outward behavior with what was going on in the heart. You need to ask God to reveal the true motives of your heart because "the heart is deceitful above all things and beyond cure" (Jer. 17:9). Consider your motive before you speak. Is it to be honest or hurtful? Are you saying no for the right reasons or to seek revenge? Are you saying yes because you want to or because you're afraid to say no? Is your comment designed to point out his or her fault and give a lecture on the solution? The following are examples of right and wrong motives.

Right motives include the following:

- To please God
- To do right
- To act in the best interest of others
- To obey God
- To take responsibility for your actions
- To allow others to bear their own consequences
- To allow others to take care of their responsibilities
- To refuse to enable
- To expose evil
- To be truthful
- To act out of love and compassion
- To be true to your beliefs and values
- To protect yourself and others

Wrong motives include the following:

- To punish and seek revenge
- To rescue (prevent someone from having to be responsible for his or her actions)
- To bear the consequences of another's behavior
- To manipulate and control
- To deceive or be dishonest
- To please someone else at the expense of hurting yourself or disobeying God

• To allow fear to dictate your choices

Motives may compete with each other. For instance, protecting someone's confidence may come before being brutally honest when answering a question. You may have to support your husband rather than an adult child. Taking care of yourself may be more important than meeting someone else's needs.

Jill's stepdaughter spends money irresponsibly. Jill wants Lynn to like her, so she gives her money. Jill's motive for giving Lynn money is to buy her love. Jill doesn't stop to consider whether she's hurting Lynn by encouraging irresponsibility, because she's concerned only with her own need to be liked. Her motive is wrong.

Amy stops by her daughter's apartment daily. She gives a reason each time, but in reality she's checking up on her daughter because she doesn't like what she's doing: drinking, dating unsaved men, and hanging out with a bad group. Amy's motive is wrong. She's checking up on her daughter dishonestly and seeking to control her.

Looking at your motives and making sure they're right, honest, and pleasing to God can simplify many of the tough decisions you have to make in difficult relationships. Your goal should be to please God rather than people (1 Thess. 2:6).

Adjust Your Expectations

Expectations are normal; everyone has them. It's reasonable to expect that people will care, be responsible, listen, pay bills, keep their word, tell the truth, show up when expected, apologize when wrong, reciprocate, and be accountable. But in difficult relationships these expectations are not fulfilled.

Difficult relationships involve people who do not have the ability or desire to do what is normally expected due to addictions, irresponsibility, mental illness, personality problems, emotional wounds, past experiences, denial, immaturity, manipulation, pride, selfishness, stubbornness, greed, resentment, lust, anger, or ignorance. By expecting something from someone who cannot or will not deliver, you're placing yourself in the position to be disappointed and resentful.

If your father is a self-centered narcissist who has always been unable to show you love, it would be foolish for you to expect him to treat you differently the next time you see him. Instead, if you accept the fact that this is how he is, you'll not be disappointed.

Many expectations come in the form of "shoulds." These are specific expectations about how things ought to be— standards you believe others should follow. Here are some examples:

- "My adult children should call me every day."
- "My parents should approve of me."
- "My mother and father should be interested in my children."
- "My brothers should help take care of Mom too."
- "My sister should get help for her addiction and mental illness."
- "My daughter should leave her alcoholic husband."

Let these predetermined ideas go if they're unreasonable for your circumstances. Solomon wrote that unfulfilled dreams make us sick (Prov. 13:12). Are you tired of being sick? Expect less. Even in prison Paul was able to say, "I have learned to be content whatever the circumstances. I know what it is to be in need, and I know what it is to have plenty" (Phil. 4:11-12). Paul let go of expectations and accepted things the way they were.

Accept Others as They Are

Just as you can accept your circumstances, you must also accept the fact that others are who they are. Paul wrote in

Rom. 15:7, "Accept one another, then, just as Christ accepted you, in order to bring praise to God."

Acceptance is an important part of being at peace with your life and the people in it. You cannot force anyone to change. An addict is an addict. An angry person is angry. Irresponsible people do irresponsible things and make bad choices. Selfish people won't care about your needs or feelings. Other people may not agree with you and may feel differently about your troubled loved one. Tolerance for their opinions and feelings is critical. You can't change them either. When you accept the facts about people, you'll begin to have energy to do more productive things like controlling your responses, making better choices, taking care of yourself and your family, and enjoying life.

Acceptance does not mean you like the situation; it means you stop trying to change things over which you have no control. You accept circumstances and people as they are so you can focus on your own choices and on changing yourself. It doesn't mean they can never change (although some people don't)—only that you can't make them.

Acknowledge the Good

Everyone needs to be appreciated, loved, and approved. Regardless of the wrong things your loved one does, there's always something positive to acknowledge. When your loved one is acting the worst is when love is most needed. Maybe all you can do is acknowledge something small: he or she looks nice, took time to stop by for a few minutes, called to say hi, or accomplished something. Maybe he or she is trying to stay sober. No matter how small, notice it and compliment it. You never know the effect the compliment will have. Approval is like a gift; it softens the receiver's heart toward you (Prov. 18:16). Try it—it can only help.

Change the Pattern

By now you're probably wondering, *If I change, will my*

loved one change? The answer is that the relationship will change when *you* change, regardless of whether or not he or she changes in the way you would like. Doing the same thing over and over and expecting different results is one definition of insanity. You must do something different, or the same patterns will continue, and the relationship may even get worse.

You're not responsible for your loved one's behavior, and he or she is not responsible for yours. But what you do affects him or her, just as what he or she does affects you. When *you* change, the *relationship* changes too. If you change your reaction, you'll be responding differently so the relationship will be different—even if your loved one doesn't know it.

As a Christian, you have the opportunity to be salt and light in every relationship (Matt. 5:13-16). Regardless of how others behave, you have a tremendous amount of influence for good or evil in all your relationships. It was God's plan that Christians stay in the world, in difficult relationships, to show His love and continue His mission (John 17:13-19). Focus on changing yourself so that you can be what God wants you to be in difficult relationships. Be a catalyst for good rather than a reactor for wrong.

DETACH WITH LOVE

*A righteous man is cautious in friendship, but the way of the
wicked leads them astray.*
—Prov. 12:26

A phone call, a look, a simple conversation, a thought
—any of these can ruin the next hour or the whole
day for you when you can't detach from your difficult relationship. If I told you there is a way for you to have a good
life regardless of what your loved one does, would you believe it? Does that seem impossible for you? The concept of
loving detachment allows you to do just that.

DETACHMENT

Detachment is about separating yourself physically, emotionally, spiritually, and mentally from situations that have a
negative effect on you. You can use detachment to avoid being led astray by the poor choices your loved one makes.

You don't have to be affected by everything your loved
one says and does. Detachment allows you to be responsible
for your own feelings, thoughts, and actions. When you detach, you're able to let your loved one be responsible for his
or her own feelings, thoughts, and actions. It allows you to
let your loved one suffer the consequences of personal
choices and take credit for successes. Detachment lets you
choose how you act rather than constantly reacting. When
you refuse to *react* to others, it's easier for you to stand back
and clearly analyze your situation. You can then choose your
behavior according to what's right, thus experiencing fewer

regrets in your life. You can make choices that are good for
you and pleasing to God.

Loving detachment is not abandoning your loved one,
and it's not indifference or lack of concern. It's treating
your loved one with love and compassion while living your
own life with dignity. Loving detachment allows you to allow
your loved one the dignity of freedom and self-responsibili-
ty. It is a respectful and loving way to treat yourself and your
loved one.

GOD DETACHES FROM US

God has given you free will that allows you to make mistakes, and He loves you no matter what you do. Yet even
with this unconditional love, He gives you boundaries, disciplines you, and permits you to suffer consequences. He has
compassion for you, but He does not step in to rescue you.
He does not excuse your sins, yet He readily extends mercy
and grace to you when you ask Him to.

But God expects repentance and change. When the woman caught in adultery came to Jesus, He looked at her with
compassion—and told her to stop sinning (John 8:1-11). He
did not excuse or condone her sin, but He held her responsible for it and gave her a chance to change directions.

You can model your loving detachment after God's.

IT'S HIS OR HER PROBLEM

Remember—your loved one is responsible for his own or
her own problems. His or her addiction, anger, drug use, inappropriate reactions, mistakes, broken relationships, and
poor choices are not problems you're accountable for. You
have been unsuccessful in forcing change to this point,
haven't you? So don't take on responsibility for fixing your
loved one. Once you realize that his or her personal choices
are beyond your control, you can separate yourself by disen-
gaging. That is the beginning of detachment.

The only exception is if your loved one suffers from a

mental illness or disability that renders him or her incapable of seeking help. Even then, however, there are areas of free choice and legal constraints that limit what you can do. If you feel responsible for an adult child because you raised that child in a difficult environment, you can admit your mistakes, make reasonable amends, and then know that your child is responsible for what he or she does with the past, present, and future. You are not responsible forever because you made mistakes.

Begin seeing your loved one's actions from a different point of view. If your parent says you never amounted to anything, say to yourself, *My worth is not determined by someone who is difficult to please.* If your son is exhibiting anger, say to yourself, *He's angry,* rather than *What did I do to make him angry?* If your spouse feels differently about how to handle your adult daughter's alcoholism, remember that your spouse is entitled to his or her opinion, and you're entitled to yours. You're not a failure because you can't fix someone or make others approve of or agree with you.

A Reason Is Not an Excuse

You may think, *He can't help it—he had a difficult childhood. She has a psychological problem. He's unsaved, so he doesn't know any better. She's been hurt in the past. He struggles with his addiction. She's in a difficult situation.* Knowing why your loved one does something does not relieve that person from responsibility for doing it, nor does it excuse the behavior. God does not excuse sin. If your daughter was hurt by the mistakes of others or struggles with a problem that wasn't her fault, you can understand and empathize and help appropriately. But if you're enabling your daughter in a destructive lifestyle because you feel sorry for her, you're harming rather than helping.

Alcoholism is a disease. That doesn't excuse a person from getting help to overcome it. It's called a disease because it can result in physical death. It is an addiction that gets progressively worse, much like other diseases. Nonetheless, alcoholics are fully responsible for taking the first drink and for the ways they hurt others when they drink. The same principle applies to other problems. Many persons who suffer from mental illness require lifelong use of medication to live normal lives but refuse to take their medication. Just because someone struggles with a problem doesn't mean he or she can't choose to do whatever it takes to make the situation better.

Brandy knew her son, Jimmy, suffered from bipolar disorder and drug abuse. She knew that many people with that illness use drugs to balance their high and low moods. She even knew that they often refuse to take their medication when they start to feel better. After watching her son struggle for 10 years with the illness, she knew it was difficult for him. Yet she had to hold him accountable for his anger and his drug use. She compassionately told him that she would support his getting help, financially and emotionally, but that if he didn't go back on his medication, control his anger, and stop the drugs, he would have to move out until he could comply.

You can know why people do what they do and still hold them accountable for their decisions—because they have the choice of getting help for their problems. If their actions are hurting others, they can do whatever it takes to change those actions. But if they don't care enough about themselves to take care of themselves, it's not likely that they'll care about others either. Your compassion is misplaced if you use it to give them an excuse to do anything they want regardless of the effect on others.

GIVE UP ENABLING

Enablers make it possible for their loved ones to continue negative behavior. They pick up the broken pieces, prevent consequences from happening, cover up, deny and pretend, keep the peace at any cost, tolerate unacceptable behavior, and take over the person's responsibilities. Enabling prevents change.

Enablers cover irresponsibility for fear of losing financial or physical security. They keep the peace so there won't be an upset. They make excuses to family and friends so no one finds out the truth. They tolerate hurtful behavior because they're afraid of the consequences if they say no. As a result, they actually prolong the problem.

God has established a law of reaping what we sow (Gal. 6:7-8). The world works on natural principles that He has established. Premarital sex may result in pregnancy or sexual disease. Abuse destroys marriages. Parents who mistreat their children don't enjoy good adult relationships with them. Drinking and driving can result in an accident and losing driving privileges. Using illegal drugs can result in jail time. People who refuse to work can't pay their bills. Enablers often prevent these natural consequences.

"If a man digs a pit, he will fall into it; if a man rolls a stone, it will roll back on him" (Prov. 26:27). Allowing your loved one to continue destructive behavior without feeling the pain of consequences actually allows the person to put off making difficult choices.

It's not easy to stop enabling. It may feel uncomfortable and scary. It probably isn't what you want to do; but it's what you *must* do. God feels the same way about it that you do: "He does not willingly bring affliction or grief to the children of men" (Lam. 3:33). But it's essential if you want to initiate change and improve your difficult relationship in the long run. However, in the short run, things may get worse because "fools despise wisdom and discipline" (Prov. 1:7).

DETACH FROM BLAME

In the Garden of Eden, Adam blamed God and Eve for

his choice to eat the forbidden fruit (Gen. 3:12-14). Eve blamed the serpent. "A man's own folly ruins his life, yet his heart rages against the LORD" (Prov. 19:3). Your loved one may rage against you and blame you for his or her foolish choices, but you must detach from it.

Blame becomes accusations: "It's your fault our son has this drug problem." "I wouldn't be a drug addict if you were a better parent." "I wouldn't have lost my job if you paid my car payment so I could get there." "I could work if you took care of the kids for me." Blame says, "You did that, so I have to do this. *You're* responsible for my actions, choices, and feelings."

Blame is a means of manipulating you and causing you to feel guilty in order to pressure you to comply with the finger-pointer's wishes. You can choose to ignore the guilt and not be manipulated, or you can accept the responsibility for your loved one's actions and be controlled. Even if you do what he or she wants, however, you'll be blamed for something else the next time he or she wants to avoid responsibility.

Blame can also be a diversionary tactic used to keep you defending yourself, allowing the real issue to be ignored. Tom knew his son's drinking was out of hand. He knew he needed to confront it and give Alex guidelines if Alex was going to continue living at home. The problem was that every time he tried to talk to Alex, Alex accused him of being angry. Tom would defend his anger and concern, but Alex didn't accept his explanation. They never got around to addressing the real issue: Alex's drinking. Alex found that blame served its purpose. When you sense that blame is being used to get you sidetracked, don't respond to the blame. Say what you need to say while ignoring the blame.

In healthy relationships, people resolve conflicts by exploring problems. In dysfunctional relationships, people are unable to resolve problems because of defensiveness, blame, insecurities, games, manipulations, immaturity, and indirect and unclear communication. When you're blamed, separate yourself from the situation, and think about the part you played in it. If the blame is legitimate, take responsibility for it. Don't apologize for things you didn't do, things you know aren't wrong, for how someone feels, or for how someone reacts to your choices. Your loved one's bad choices are not your responsibility.

DETACH FROM ANGER

Just as you detach from blame, you must also detach from anger. Prov. 29:22 says, "An angry man stirs up dissension, and a hot-tempered one commits many sins." Prov. 22:24-25 advises, "Do not make friends with a hot-tempered man, do not associate with one easily angered, or you may learn his ways and get yourself ensnared." Don't argue or engage an angry person. Prov. 15:1 tells us, "A gentle answer turns away wrath, but a harsh word stirs up anger." Walk away. Hold your tongue. Answer gently. Listen quietly. Continue the discussion when things have cooled down. As Prov. 20:3 says, "It is to a man's honor to avoid strife, but every fool is quick to quarrel."

Anger is damaging to you emotionally, spiritually, and physically. It doesn't feel good to know that someone is angry with you. But it's the other person's feeling, and you don't have to fix it or defend your innocence. Remember that anger is often an emotional cover-up for something else: hurt, insecurity, fear, guilt, sadness, disappointment, and shame. Because anger is damaging, you always have the right to walk away from it. Just because someone's angry at you does not mean that you did something wrong. Even if you're guilty as charged, you can still walk away and wait to apologize when you're not being mistreated.

Phil was always angry. Both his wife and son tried to listen and appease him. They tried to defend themselves. Nothing worked. Finally they realized that they could not change his anger and that they didn't cause it. They decided to stay away from him when he was angry.

Always protect yourself when dealing with violent people. Make alternate plans to ensure your safety. You have a right to walk away from anyone who's hurting you or making you feel unsafe.

DETACH FROM MOODS

Detachment allows you to separate yourself from destructive moods. Moods are catching. If your loved one is uptight and anxious; you become uptight and anxious. If he or she is miserable, you're miserable. If your daughter is angry, you feel angry. If your parent is unhappy, you're unhappy. You can't make your loved one change his or her mood. Moods are typically irrational and nonresponsive to reason. Your challenge is not to change the mood but to keep that mood from becoming yours.

It wasn't easy to watch Sherry's depressions, but Linda did it for 11 years, attempting to help her daughter feel better. Sherry refused to get help, and nothing Linda said got through to her. Linda noticed that she felt depressed and defeated herself when Sherry went into her states of lethargy and isolation. Linda decided to show Sherry love during her depressions but to detach from the compulsion she felt to change Sherry's mood. Instead, Linda purposefully did things that kept her busy and happy.

Detachment allows you to take the focus off others and allows you to have a good day whether or not your loved one is having one.

DETACH FROM THREATS

"Better to meet a bear robbed of her cubs than a fool in his folly" (Prov. 17:12). If someone does not want to be accountable, he or she will react strongly to confrontation. The purpose of the threat is to control your behavior and get you to back down. Your natural tendency is probably to panic, taking the threat seriously. If you back down, the threat is a success.

Ron didn't want to be responsible for his own bills or his hostile attitude toward his parents. Every time they tried to discuss it with him, he threatened to move out and never see them again. For a long time, Frank and Joyce backed down, afraid that if they pushed him he would leave. Finally they realized that Ron's threats were preventing him and them from dealing with the problems. They decided to ignore the threats and confront the issues.

As long as you're doing what you know is right, ignore threats. Threats are not action. As long as someone is threatening, he or she is not following through. Threats are empty words. The exception is if the threat is to harm someone and you have reason to believe it might actually happen. In that case, you need to do what it takes to protect innocent people, including yourself.

DETACH FROM OTHERS' FAILURES

It's hard to see people we care about suffer because of their mistakes, poor choices, bad decisions, and purposeful wrongdoing. When we're successful at detaching with love, we offer support and show concern but stop short of jumping in to fix the situation for our loved one.

Jackie's daughter has two small children from different fathers and is currently living with a drug-addicted boyfriend. Brenda frequently calls Jackie to complain about the problems and ask for money and help with the children. The latest problem was her boyfriend's arrest. She asked Jackie for bail money, but Jackie refused, expressing her heartfelt concern for Brenda and all she was going through. She truthfully said, "Honey, I love you. I know your relationship with Stan is full of problems. I hope you will eventually have a good relationship so that you and the children are truly happy, but I'm not going to bail him out."

DETACH FROM CRISES

Let your loved one deal with the natural consequences of his or her choices. Don't cover up, make excuses, lie, explain, manipulate, set up, arrange, or do anything to prevent the crisis from happening. Prov. 19:19 says, "A hot-tempered man must pay the penalty; if you rescue him, you will have to do it again." If your daughter won't work, don't pay her bills. If your brother hits his wife, don't post his bail. If your father drives drunk, don't drive him to work or fix his car after he wrecks. Don't baby-sit your neighbor's children while their parents stay out partying. Don't call the boss to make an excuse for your hung-over husband. Don't pay your friend's electric bill because she gambled away her paycheck; let the lights be turned off.

On the other hand, don't *create* a crisis to force change. That would be just as destructive as preventing a crisis. Don't call your daughter-in-law and tell her everything you know about your son (unless it's to protect her and the children). Don't disown a loved one because of an addiction. Don't threaten to never see your grandchildren because it isn't on your terms. Don't call the police when you know someone is drinking and driving. Don't angrily blurt out how everyone in the family feels about the difficult person.

Take care of yourself and the things you're responsible for, and let others take care of themselves. Nothing lasts forever, and crises pass. There's a time for everything (Eccles. 3:1-8). "Weeping may remain for a night, but rejoicing comes in the morning" (Ps. 30:5).

TAKE CARE OF YOUR RESPONSIBILITIES

Do not attempt to detach by neglecting your responsibilities or the relationship. Do the things you're supposed to do and need to do—whether or not your loved one fulfills his or her responsibilities. Don't retaliate or punish in any way. Baby-sit your grandchildren when you want to, not because you feel guilty if you don't. Enjoy buying gifts for special occasions but not because you're covering for irresponsibility. Help out once in a while because you want to. Help when it's genuinely needed unless it enables destructive behavior. Support efforts to improve. You can still be a loving mother, father, daughter, son, sister, brother, grandparent, friend, uncle, aunt, or cousin and detach from that person's dysfunction. Do what you want to do because you care. Don't do what you feel compelled to do out of a need to rescue. There *is* a difference.

BE COURTEOUS AND KIND

Communication in dysfunctional relationships is often full of sarcasm, mumbled comments, snide remarks, silence, withdrawal, personal attacks, accusations, threats, name-calling, anger, lectures, interrogation, and putdowns. The tone of voice and interaction style communicates contempt, hostility, and disdain.

No matter how bad the relationship has become, common courtesy changes the tone. "Let your conversation be always full of grace, seasoned with salt, so that you may know how to answer everyone" (Col. 4:6). If you have a habit of speaking in a rude, demeaning, or unpleasant tone, learn to speak courteously, even when you don't feel like it. Remember to say *Please, Thank you,* and *You're welcome.* However, courtesy is more than mere politeness; it's an attitude that communicates respect and kindness and bestows dignity on everyone it touches. It changes even the most difficult relationships.

DON'T BE CONTROLLED

Difficult people are often controlling people who want to have power over others. They don't understand give and take, equality, and mutuality in a relationship. They may not have your best interest in mind, even though you have theirs. They operate in a "win-lose" mode rather than a "win-win" mode. They may see you as their adversary, resulting in their actions being designed to defeat you. You can feel this power play in passive and subtle ways as well as obvious ways, though it's not always easy to put your finger on. If you feel manipulated, outwitted, confused, and controlled, you're probably involved with a controlling person.

Don't try to manipulate back or outsmart them. You'll lose. Instead, be aware of the game and refuse to play. Don't explain your behavior, try to rationalize, try to convince, defend yourself, argue, appease, accept abuse, or accept blame. Deal as directly and honestly as possible, always keeping the focus on yourself. Keep the discussion short so you don't get too involved, and work on setting boundaries.

DON'T ARGUE WITH THE PROBLEM

When your loved one is under the influence of alcohol or drugs, in a "dry drunk," raging, behaving irrationally, in denial, in a mood for whatever reason or whatever it is he or she does, don't argue with him or her. "A fool finds no pleasure in understanding but delights in airing his own opinions" (Prov. 18:2). Fools refuse to be reproved. Prov. 23:9 advises, "Do not speak to a fool, for he will scorn the wisdom of your words."

Have you ever found yourself arguing with someone who was in an unreasonable state and found yourself acting just as unreasonable? That's what happens when you attempt to answer someone who's not capable of rational reason.

That doesn't mean that there will never be a time to state the truth. There will be a time to speak. As Prov. 26:5 says, "Answer a fool according to his folly, or he will be wise in his own eyes." However, that time is not when your loved one is in an unreasonable state. Instead of arguing or trying to convince him or her in the heat of the battle, wait until he or she is sober, calm, humble, and receptive. Use wisdom to determine when you should speak. But always remember—you can't force him or her to agree with you or to accept what you say. You have to say it and detach from the reaction.

Here are some practical ways to respond to a loved one who wants to argue with you. You can say any of the following:

- "No."
- "Yes."
- "Maybe."
- "You could be right."
- "I'll think about that."
- "Could be."
- "Thank you."
- "I hear you."
- "I understand."
- "That's your opinion."
- "I might."
- "Possibly."
- "Good point."

These answers are all short and end a conversation in a gracious way. They distance you from the words and anger. In other words, they help you detach rather than get you hooked into arguing.

DON'T BELIEVE LIES

Difficult people are dysfunctional and often hold distorted ideas and perceptions and unreasonable rules and expectations about how relationships should be and how you should act. These result in lies and mistruths. The discussions and arguments you have with dysfunctional people may make your head spin and make you feel as though you're crazy. You may find yourself repeatedly arguing things that don't make sense. You must refuse to believe distortions and lies. You can't let an unhealthy or unstable person determine your view of things. When you hear lies and distortions, fight against those ideas, and refuse to accept them as truths, using truth, righteousness, and the shield of faith to stop the lies (Eph. 6:14, 16). Lies may come from the need to blame you for the problems, insecurity, the need to control you, misperceptions, emotional brokenness, deep wounds, false beliefs, denial, and a willingness to inflict pain. Even though these comments hurt, you can choose whether you want to believe them.

One way to detach from disturbing and irrational comments is to remember that it's the problem talking. How can you listen to someone whose thinking is distorted and still take everything he or she says seriously? "A false witness will perish, and whoever listens to him will be destroyed" (Prov. 21:28). Detachment helps you realize that you don't have to accept your loved one's words as the truth; you don't have to let yourself be destroyed by them. You can choose not to take every comment personally. "Like a fluttering sparrow or a darting swallow, an undeserved curse does not come to rest" (Prov. 26:2).

DON'T GET HOOKED

Don't get hooked by letting your buttons be pushed. A button is anything that makes you react. A hook is anything that pulls you into the battle. It may be an attitude, an action, a look, a response, or a subject that you react to every time it's brought up. It may be a phrase or response that triggers a negative answer or deliberately ignoring something that's important to you. Regardless of what it is, you'll know it's your button because you'll sense an instant reaction in yourself.

Difficult people want to push your buttons and hook you into playing their game on their terms. Why? So you'll react. Then they can point the finger at you and blame you for their actions. Sometimes they just want you to be as upset as they are. When you begin to change, you'll notice that they try even harder to hook you, because they want you to react in familiar ways. Change in you produces insecurity and fear in them. When you detach, the attempts to make you react may increase, so be prepared.

Live Your Life

How do you detach? By living your life one moment at a time. You have things you need to do. Do them. When your thoughts wander into the past or future, pull them back to where you are at that moment. Enjoy the simple things. Pay attention to life. Focus your mind on God's creation. Notice how the wind, sun, or cold feels on your skin. Look at the flowers and trees. Look at your grandchildren or children. Listen to them. Play with them. Hear them. Pay attention to what people say to you. Jesus told us to keep our thoughts on the moment (Matt. 6:34).

Keeping your thoughts on what you're doing at the moment is a powerful way to put detachment into practice. At the end of the day, you will have accomplished what you needed to do, and you'll feel a lot better about yourself and your life.

Act As If

Detachment takes practice. At first you may catch yourself saying the wrong thing and stop midsentence to apologize. You may have to walk away from conversations when everything in you wants to argue. You may even have to leave to keep yourself from reacting. You may feel paralyzed with fear and feel as if it's a betrayal when you let your loved one suffer the consequences of his or her actions. The first time you do something different, it may not feel right. That's OK. Do it anyway.

"Acting as if" means choosing how to act and allowing your feelings to come later. It's a way to practice good behavior. It's not pretending or denial. You act detached by doing things that show you're detached. You have to put detachment into practice before you feel it. Eventually you'll begin to feel it.

Kristin didn't want to be involved with her parents' arguments. When she visited them, they both tried to get her to take sides. She had always been their mediator, explaining one to the other, feeling responsible for fixing them. The next time she visited, Kristin decided to try detachment. She said with a smile, "I love both of you, but you're going to have to work out your own arguments." Inside she feared their reaction and felt she was letting them down, but she didn't show it. Before long, they accepted her refusal, and she felt free of her mediator role.

Actions sometimes speak louder than words. You have probably spoken so many words to your difficult person that he or she has tuned you out. He or she may notice a change in your actions before listening to a change in your words.

DETACH WITH LOVE

Detaching with love means you give your loved one the dignity to be an adult and make decisions without your approval and control, realizing that he or she is an imperfect human struggling with problems but doing the best he or she can do for now, even if it appears evil and destructive to you. Have compassion for the struggle, the past hurts, and the pain. See your loved one not as an evil person but as a sick, hurting child of God who needs help. This allows you to replace hatred and contempt with kindness and courtesy.

"Do not repay evil with evil" or return the "insult with insult" (1 Pet. 3:9). Do not retaliate. You can genuinely bring a cup of water in Christ's name and treat your loved one with dignity even when you're being mistreated (Rom. 12:17-21).

Take care of your own responsibilities, not your loved one's. Even though you feel compassion, don't excuse your loved one's bad behavior. Don't allow yourself to be used and mistreated. "In the paths of the wicked lie thorns and snares, but he who guards his soul stays far from them" (Prov. 22:5). Detachment guards your soul. It's part of taking care of yourself.

NURTURE YOURSELF

No one ever hated his own body, but he feeds and cares for it, just as Christ does the church. —Eph. 5:29

D o you use any of these excuses for not taking care of yourself?

- "I don't have the time."
- "I don't have the money."
- "I'm too overwhelmed with my problems."
- "I don't have fun anyway."
- "I don't want to be selfish."
- "I don't care about myself."

You fill many roles: child, parent, grandchild, sibling, in-law, cousin, friend, coworker, employee, citizen, church member, nephew or niece, uncle or aunt, neighbor, volunteer, and child of God. All relationships require energy and time, but difficult relationships require more than their share of time and energy. The more demands that are placed on you, the more you need to take care of yourself. If you're not healthy in every aspect of your life, you can't give yourself in a healthy way to relationships.

Taking care of yourself does not mean you callously ignore others while you're on a self-seeking mission. It's about learning to nurture and revitalize yourself so that you can give to others—in the right way. It's about becoming all God created you to be so that you can use your talents to glorify Him.

Have you pushed your own needs aside for so long that you don't even know what you would like to do if you had the chance? Ask yourself these questions:

- "What did I used to like to do?"
- "What do I find myself dreaming about?"
- "What do I regret not doing?"
- "What do I envy about other people?"
- "What things motivate and interest me?"
- "If I could do anything I want, what would it be?"
- "As a low-energy person, what would motivate me to action?"
- "As a high-energy or high-stress person, what would relax me?"
- "What looks like fun when I see others doing it?"

Your answers should give you a few ideas of things you can do that will help you relax, discover and grow your gifts and talents, improve your self-esteem, enjoy your life, and glorify God.

IT'S NOT SELFISH

Others may accuse you of being selfish when you begin to take care of yourself. "Selfish" is defined in this case as doing anything for yourself rather than for the dysfunctional system. When you begin to make healthy changes and take care of yourself, you'll stir up the insecurities and fears in your difficult loved one. Remember: change in you changes the complexion of the difficult relationship.

You may be told that your needs and problems don't matter compared to the one who has all the problems, because your needs and concerns are less urgent and intense. How can you compare your everyday needs to someone who's on and off drugs or suicidal? You can't compete with drama, turmoil, emotional extremes, and uncertainty.

Maybe you don't need anyone to tell you that you're selfish because you believe you shouldn't nurture yourself anyway. Or maybe the accusation that you're selfish makes you feel guilty. If you've been in a dysfunctional relationship for a significant amount of time, you've probably accepted the idea that you should never put your needs before the needs of others. Christians commonly make this mistake too. As a result, you may have come to believe that you're significant only when taking care of the needs of others. This belief feeds the idea that you're responsible for other people. You're not.

Your needs are just as important as your loved one's needs. Make the conscious choice to treat yourself that way.

Lena was raised in a dysfunctional family. Her mother took care of her husband and the children. She never did anything for herself, believing a woman's place is in the home. Lena was raised in the church where she also heard the message that she should love others, not herself. She remembers being told, "Nice Christian girls don't ask for things. Be content. Help others." When Lena wanted to go away to college, her mother and father accused her of being selfish and deserting the family. They said she needed to stay home and help her mom with the younger children, so she stayed home. As a married woman, she feels guilty every time she thinks of doing something for herself apart from her husband and daughters.

Difficult people may not care about your best interest. Addicts and other dysfunctional people are self-centered. While your loved one accuses you of being selfish, he or she is exhibiting that very trait himself or herself but does not recognize it.

TAKE CARE OF YOUR OWN EMOTIONAL NEEDS

Taking care of your own emotional needs means you attend to emotional issues as they surface. It's important not to deny your emotions, because that can do inward damage to your body and your relationships with others and God. Unresolved emotional wounds from the past affect how you interact with others. If you don't pay attention to your feelings and process them as they arise, they'll pile up, and you'll find yourself dumping your emotional garbage on others whether you want to or not.

Talk about your emotions with a friend, counselor, sponsor, or mentor. It should be someone who will listen, help you see things clearly, and will be honest and willing to gently point out your weaknesses. It should be someone you admire for his or her emotional and spiritual maturity and preferably has experienced similar problems, enabling compassionate understanding.

Another way to take care of your emotions is to guard them by tempering your reactions to people, places, and things.

After arguments you're exhausted mentally, emotionally, physically, and spiritually. You then have a big mess to clean up: apologies, regrets, anger, embarrassment, and guilt. Refuse to react to others, and refuse to allow your emotions to explode. That's taking care of yourself.

You may not be an outward reactor. Maybe you just respond inside with enormous emotional explosions of guilt, fear, worry, anxiety, tension, and sadness. Those inside eruptions are just as damaging. You need to deal with those emotions by talking about them with someone you trust and by understanding what your emotions are telling you about your life.

Emotions are not meant to dictate your actions—they're signs meant to tell you what's going on inside. Identify them, understand them, process them, interpret them, and then decide what you want to do with them. Taking care of your emotional needs insures that you'll not allow emotions to sabotage your life.

TAKE CARE OF YOUR PHYSICAL NEEDS

God created your body to need rest and rejuvenation. Part of understanding that you are "fearfully and wonderfully made" (Ps. 139:14) is to have respect for the body God gave you by taking care of it (Eph. 5:29). When you allow yourself to be run down, you won't be able to handle life's challenges as well as when you're physically strong.

It's also very easy to get resentful toward others when you're overextended. Renee found herself angry with her husband and adult sons for not helping around the house. She was involved in so many projects that she was exhausted every night. She resented anyone who was sitting down doing nothing. She finally realized that she was choosing to do too much and needed to make a choice to rest. She also realized that she needed to ask for help when she needed it.

You also need to take time for exercise. It may be walking, joining a gym, golfing, doing aerobics, swimming, or participating in any other sport. Choose one you like so you'll continue doing it. Exercise increases your energy, makes your thinking clearer, and improves your health. It also helps you overcome depression.

Pay attention to your nutritional needs by eating a balanced diet. Limit sugar and simple carbohydrates (pasta, white bread, and crackers). Eating right keeps your weight down and gives you more energy. Skipping meals decreases your energy and ability to think clearly. In addition to a good diet, you may need vitamins. When you feel good, you'll have a more positive outlook toward life.

You may ignore your own health needs either because you don't have the time to deal with them or don't think you're important. You have to learn to value your physical health. How will you have anything to give to others if you're sick? Even simple physical imbalances can make you feel as though you cannot handle life. God made you a steward over your body. He wants you to take care of the temple that's the dwelling place of His Spirit (1 Cor. 3:16-17).

There are times when antidepressants and antianxiety medication are necessary. Don't use drugs as a substitute for dealing with your problems, but don't feel that you're weak if you need them. Severe depression and anxiety, as well as many other mental imbalances, require medication to be corrected. Talk to your doctor or counselor. Counselors cannot prescribe drugs but can help you make a decision on whether you need them.

When you're tired you're less tolerant. Try to do less on the days you're physically exhausted. Those are not the days to take on a big project, make a big decision, or have that big confrontation. Anxiety and depression interfere with regular restful sleep. Lack of exercise can also cause poor sleep. If you have sleep problems, try to deal with the underlying cause. Regular nighttime routines help to overcome insomnia.

Sue noticed that when she was depressed, she ignored her physical needs. When she put a priority on taking care of herself, she felt less negative about life and more positive about herself. She was also more assertive in her relationships when she felt good and less affected by others' moods.

Taking care of your physical needs affects all areas of your life and relationships.

TAKE CARE OF YOUR RELATIONAL NEEDS

You have relationships with many different people, but you probably find that your difficult relationships dominate your thoughts, attention, and emotion, draining most of your energy. Parents ignore other children while focusing on the troubled child. Husbands and wives in difficult marriages ignore their children. Husbands and wives ignore each other while focusing on a wayward child. Grandparents cater to one troubled grandchild while ignoring others. Friends focus most of their attention on a hurting friend by allowing the conversation to focus on one person's problems. When you learn to take care of yourself, you begin to pay attention to all your relationships.

If you envision all your relationships as God-given, you'll view them differently. All the people God has allowed to be in your life have significance. Some are there to love, encourage, and bless you. Others are there for you to minister to. Some carry a special responsibility, demanding a high priority, like your spouse and children (1 Cor. 7:32-34; 1 Tim. 5:8). Your goal is to be a good steward of each relationship. It's not God's will that you ignore those He has put within your circle of influence. As Rom. 12:5 says, "In Christ we who are many form one body, and each member belongs to all the others." There are many people in your life for you to enjoy relationships with.

Friendships are important. Men need men, and women need women. There's a special camaraderie, affirmation, and identification between members of the same sex that's necessary at all stages of life. Who else understands menopause, hormones, wrinkles, motherhood, and PMS other than women? Who else understands locker room humor, sports mania, cars, testosterone, and balding other than men? Find friendships where you can have fun and get emotional support.

Don't spend your life grieving over what you don't have in your family or marriage when you can forge other relationships with strong bonds and emotional ties that can allow you to give and receive love. The apostle Paul had many friends, some closer than others (Col. 4:7-15). He considered Timothy to be a son (1 Tim. 1:2). Jesus asked John, "the disciple whom he loved," to take care of His mother, Mary, at His death (John 19:26-27). You can have deep relationships with people outside your family that can even substitute for what you're missing or missed with your blood relatives. "There is a friend who sticks closer than a brother" (Prov. 18:24).

Taking care of relationships helps you feel good about yourself. When you know you're taking care of the important things and giving and receiving love, you'll feel connected and at peace.

TAKE CARE OF YOUR SPIRITUAL NEEDS

You may neglect your spiritual needs due to a lack of time, of misplaced priorities, or because you're struggling spiritually.

Difficult relationships stir up so many emotions and conflicting desires that at times you may feel unchristian. There were times when I felt like a hypocrite in church until I understood that the weaker I was, the nearer God was to me. As Ps. 34:18 says, "The LORD is close to the brokenhearted and saves those who are crushed in spirit." Jesus said He had come to call sinners—not the righteous (Matt. 9:13). I often wondered if God really wanted to hear my worship when I had so much ugliness and turmoil in my heart. I learned to offer a sacrifice of praise in spite of how I felt.

I also felt confused reading the Bible when I was struggling with deep emotions and uncertainty regarding my difficult relationships. At these times, I found comfort in reading Psalms, Proverbs, and encouraging devotionals. David was honest in the Psalms about his struggles with intense emotions: depression, despair, confusion, envy, anger, betrayal, fear, insecurity, distrust, lust, grief, disappointment, and worry. He told God just how he felt. Proverbs also has common-sense wisdom easily absorbed in one-verse nuggets.

Sometimes confusion results from reading the Bible and thinking that every verse is literally God's specific warning or promise to you. Instead, read the Bible for its universal truths without trying to personalize every verse.

Realistically assess what you can read consistently, since it's better to meditate on a single verse or chapter each day than to read ten chapters once a week. Knowledge of the Bible helps you grow in wisdom, something you definitely need in difficult relationships.

Praise music can be very healing when you're discouraged and confused. God seems closer, and your spirit is nourished and fed. Heb. 10:25 places importance on Christians meeting together to encourage each other. Do something that connects you to other Christians. Join a Bible study and get more involved at your church.

Prayer nurtures you through a relationship with your Heavenly Father. If you're discouraged because you don't feel as if your prayers are answered, use your prayer time to talk to God about what's going on in your life. Prayer deepens your relationship with God, aligns your will to His, reduces anxiety, and helps you trust Him. Prayer for your enemies helps you to forgive and let go of resentments (Matt. 5:44). Ask God for wisdom, discernment, guidance, strength to do what's right, and your specific daily needs. Paul told us to "pray continually" (1 Thess. 5:17).

If you're struggling with anger, disillusionment, and confusion toward God over the circumstances in your life and your loved one's life, you need to deal with those feelings. God is not shocked by your admission—after all, He already knows. These feelings often come from misperceptions about Christianity, namely that God promises that everything will be good and easy. That's not the case. Instead, you've been promised trials, tribulations, struggles, and sufferings (James 1:2-4). Many assume that God will make everything turn out good, right, and just and are surprised when that's not the case. In Ps. 73 Asaph wrote of a similar confusion. He got disillusioned with God when he saw the wicked prospering and the righteous suffering—until God showed him that everything turns out right and just in the end. God has not promised to make anyone choose salvation and righteousness. However, He does draw people toward Him (John 12:32) through His Holy Spirit, disciplines them to bring them to repentance (Heb. 12:5-6), and lovingly protects—especially those who are His own (Ps. 91).

TAKE CARE OF YOUR MENTAL NEEDS

Taking care of your mental needs involves using the mind God has given you by learning and expanding your knowledge and abilities. God wants us to love and serve Him with our minds (Matt. 22:37). You can take care of your mental needs by following the news, reading books, volunteering, getting a part-time job, taking a college or adult education course, or learning a new craft or skill.

Another way to take care of yourself is to pay close attention to your thoughts, because thoughts define a person (Prov. 23:7). Your thoughts are the precursors to your attitudes, behavior, emotions, and interpretations. Your thoughts are your beliefs—the ideas and perceptions you form about the world. Changing your thoughts is a powerful way to change your life and relationships. Paul said that when he was a child he thought like a child, so he acted like a child (1 Cor. 13:11). Your heart is the center of your being, the essence of everything you are. The words of your mouth come from what's inside your mind and heart (Matt. 12:34-36).

Become aware of your thoughts or self-talk. Prov. 4:23 says, "Above all else, guard your heart, for it is the well-spring of life." Your self-talk comes from your heart and consists of the dialogue in your head. It's what you tell yourself about you, life, and others, providing you with a frame of reference for all the events of your life. Self-talk can be positive or negative. It can set you up to succeed or fail. It can keep you stuck or set you free.

Here are some examples of negative self-talk:
- "I'm a failure. I'll never amount to anything."
- "People have to approve of me, or I can't handle it."
- "I can't handle it if my loved one doesn't change."
- "It's my fault when others fail."

Here are some examples of positive self-talk:
- "I'm not a failure. God has a plan for my life regardless of what other people have said about me."

- "I can't please everyone all the time. Disapproval may not be comfortable, but I'll survive it."
- "I'll feel sad if my loved one doesn't change, but I'll continue to live my life, and with God's help, I can handle anything."
- "My loved one has the responsibility to live his [her] life. It doesn't mean I failed if wrong choices are made."

Is negative self-talk impacting the way you see yourself? God does not want you defeated by anything. You're able to conquer anything with God's help and love (Rom. 8:37-39). Don't let your thoughts defeat you.

USE YOUR TALENTS

Talents include your life, time, money, abilities, experiences, relationships, gifts, knowledge, and opportunities. In other words, everything you have and do is an opportunity to do something for God.

Even though you already feel overwhelmed, helping others is good for you. There are many areas you can help in: teaching Sunday School; working in the nursery; volunteering in community and charitable organizations like a nursing home, unwed mothers' home, or homeless shelter; or helping a friend, family member, neighbor, or coworker in time of need. It can be little things like giving someone a ride, making dinner, picking up a child, offering an encouragement, sharing a good tape or book, or fixing something broken. It may even be listening to someone else in a difficult relationship and giving encouragement and wisdom from your own experiences.

Helping others balances your concerns and keeps you from being too self-centered. You're responsible for what you do with your talents (Matt. 25:14-30), including your insight, experience, and opportunities. Instead of putting off serving God until after your relationship problems are resolved, use them fully today.

Developing your talents also includes discovering who you are and the special gifts you have to give to others. You may have such low self-esteem that you think you have nothing to give. That's simply not true. God gave you gifts, and He doesn't want you to compare your gift with those of others, thinking you're less important (1 Cor. 12). He wants you to be everything He has created you to be.

Learn to relax and have fun. It doesn't have to be an expensive vacation. You can simply take a walk in the park; see a play; have lunch with a friend; get a manicure, pedicure, facial, or massage; have a cup of coffee or tea; read a fun novel; take a bubble bath; go shopping; go to the beach or park; go bike-riding; go to a movie; play a game; play sports; start a hobby; or anything else fun to you. Do things with your children: play ball, swing, color a picture, or build a sandcastle. Try something new. At first you may have difficulty having fun—you may even feel guilty. But before you know it, you'll be having fun and liking it!

Solomon came to the conclusion that God wanted him to enjoy life, calling it "a gift of God" when he was able to find satisfaction (Eccles. 5:18-20). Fun pleases God.

SAY YES AND NO

When you're asked to do something, you can say either yes or no. How do you know which is right? It depends on your needs and motives. Are you saying yes when you really want to say no? Then learn to be truthful and say no, especially when saying yes will leave you feeling resentful and angry. Jesus said to "simply let your 'Yes' be 'Yes,' and your 'No,' 'No'" (Matt. 5:37).

Accept the little things others do for you. Don't turn down gifts from your difficult loved one even if you're upset about other things. Allow others to do something nice for you the best way they know how. Taking gifts does not mean you approve of everything else, nor does it mean you owe anything. Accept them graciously, taking care of yourself in the process. The only exception is if accepting the gift seems immoral to you or is going to be used manipulatively to harm you or someone else.

Here are some additional examples.

Say no—

- When you want to say no.
- When you'll resent saying yes.
- When saying yes will cause emotional, spiritual, or mental harm to you or your family.
- When saying yes will put your priorities in jeopardy.
- When you feel obligated and are afraid to say no.

Say yes—

- When you want to say yes.
- When it's the right thing to do.
- When it's a new challenge, even if you feel afraid.

MAKE GOOD DECISIONS

Decisions are often complicated and overwhelming in the midst of difficult relationships. You often distrust your perceptions, opinions, and decision-making abilities, especially since many decisions have unpleasant consequences.

Seek advice, make sure you're obeying God's Word, pray, and then use your best reasoning, trusting God to lead you. God works all things for good in your life (Rom. 8:28) and "will make your paths straight" (Prov. 3:5-6), even if your decision appears to be wrong in hindsight.

Don't make decisions when you're angry or in the middle of a crisis. Wait until things have calmed down, since decisions made in the midst of crises often turn out to be empty threats or bad decisions. Talk over your decisions with other people, but remember: you're the one who has to do what your heart and conscience tell you, because you have to live with the outcome.

KEEP A JOURNAL

Journaling is a tool to help you understand your emotions, your thoughts, your attitudes, and God's working in your life. It helps you let go of your past, gain understanding in your present circumstances, and clarify confusing issues. It helps you recognize patterns in your difficulties. It's also a record of significant turning points or events. Writing down important events, conversations, and insights helps validate your perceptions. When I doubted my feelings and perceptions and felt confused, I wrote out my thoughts and fears and then countered them on paper with truth and God's promises.

Journaling can be a measuring stick to monitor your growth or lack of growth. You can journal new insights about your life, relationships with others, and relationship with the Lord. Keeping notes of things God is teaching you and writing lists of things you're thankful for helps you focus on your relationship with Him.

WATCH PRIORITIES

Life is demanding, even without difficult relationships. Establish a way to determine your priorities to prevent yourself from being overwhelmed. Try writing a list of everything you need to do, and number them in order of importance. Things with a deadline come first, as well as things that are related to health and safety.

Accept the very real possibility that you may not be able to do it all. Do what you can, and let the rest go—the urgent things are not always the most important. Housework can usually wait, and errands can often be put off. Spending necessary time with family is usually something that does not feel urgent but is very important.

If you have trouble taking care of yourself physically, emotionally, mentally, and spiritually, put those things on your list too. Make plans ahead of time to do fun things, such as spending time with loved ones and friends and taking part in church activities. Write them on your calendar, since you'll be more likely to do them once you feel you're committed.

Jesus warned the religious leaders of his day that they were paying too much attention to unimportant things while neglecting "the more important matters of the law—justice, mercy and faithfulness" (Matt. 23:23). Doing things that lead to righteousness is always a priority (Matt. 6:33).

KEEP IT SIMPLE

In order to counter the tendency to do too much, you have to choose to keep it simple by deliberately taking the simple way rather than the complicated way—especially when you're feeling overwhelmed. It can mean fixing an easy dinner instead of a four-course meal, buying a gift certificate rather than shopping for a gift, having a small party instead of a large one, wearing clothes that are easy to wash and maintain (that means not ironing), paying someone to do a task instead of doing it yourself, or having a child's party at the skating rink where virtually everything is done for you. Your motive is not to be lazy—it's to take care of yourself so your life stays manageable.

RESPECT YOURSELF

Treat yourself with respect, and know you deserve to be treated respectfully by people in your life. People will treat you better when they see you respect yourself and expect to be honored. My middle daughter put a sign on her door when she was in junior high school. It said, "I am Rachel. You will treat me with respect." She had good self-esteem, expecting honorable treatment from family, friends, and eventually her husband. The Prov. 31 woman was "clothed with strength and dignity" (v. 25). Her husband and children treated her well, and others praised her. Her husband was also respected by his family and outsiders. Nurturing yourself is the way you treat yourself with respect. It's an important part of improving your life.

LIVE YOUR LIFE

You may feel guilty about living your life and enjoying it when someone you love is in so much pain. It may dampen your enthusiasm for otherwise pleasurable activities. In order to take care of yourself, you'll have to learn that it's not just OK but that it's good for you to enjoy life even though your loved one is hurting. It doesn't mean that you don't care—it means you recognize that your life is not conditionally related to another person's choices.

FACE YOUR FEARS

When I am afraid, I will trust in you. —Ps. 56:3

I f you're in a difficult relationship, you probably have many fears. You face all sorts of "What ifs"—"What if he does it again?" "What if she gets angry?" "What if she cuts off the relationship?" "What if he gets hurt or hurts someone else?" "What if he loses his job or family?" "What if they disapprove of me?" "What if the rest of the family finds out?" "What if she can't take care of her responsibilities?" "What if I make a wrong decision?"

Fear is a distressing emotion caused by real or imagined impending danger, evil, or pain and underlies and directs many of your decisions. Fear is what motivates you to move out of the way of a train or bus or to go to the doctor when you feel a lump in your breast. Fear can also impede you from telling someone the truth, making changes in yourself, setting boundaries, or doing what you know is right.

Anxiety is distress or uneasiness that's caused by fear. It's anxiety that weighs you down and results in associated nervousness manifested by butterflies in the stomach, edginess, irritability, inability to cope or make decisions, inability to concentrate, inability to sleep, and a feeling of being out of control.

FEAR IS NOT A SIN

David talked often in the Psalms about being afraid. He acknowledged his fear and asked God for comfort and deliverance. It's what you do with the fear that can turn it into something that leads you to depend on God or something that leads you away from God. Jesus repeatedly directed the disciples to turn their fear into faith by trusting Him rather than reacting to fear with worry and anxiety. (See Matt. 14:22-32; John 6:16-21; Luke 8:22-25; Phil. 4:6.)

Consider these examples: Your 18-year-old son in the army is sent into an active war zone to do combat. Your husband is drinking beer with his friends and driving motorcycles. You have a breast lump the doctor labels as suspicious. Your mother tells you she has cancer. Your spouse asks for a divorce. You have to discuss an issue with someone that you know is a touchy subject. It's natural to feel fear in those circumstances.

The thing that matters most is what you do with the fear. You can project into the future, fall apart, and let the fear direct your decisions—or you can face it and choose to give your fears to God. Jane knew she had to tell her son to move out. He refused to work and came home drunk often. She felt fearful and anxious but chose to do what was right and trust God with the outcome.

SPECIFIC FEARS

As you read through a few of the common fears experienced by people in difficult relationships, try to identify the ones that affect your decisions and actions. Once you identify your fears, you'll be better equipped to deal with them and prevent them from affecting your decisions and ruling your life.

Fear of Your Loved One's Reaction

Your loved one may criticize, react angrily, manipulate, threaten, retaliate, blame, throw out guilt, verbally abuse, argue, withdraw, refuse to cooperate, ignore, pout, complain, turn to others, or punish. You know which of those reactions you fear and how they affect you. Pay attention to those specific instances in which you find yourself doing something you don't want to do or not doing something you want to do because you're afraid of a reaction.

Helen's dad verbally berated her in front of her children. She tolerated it because she knew that when she confronted him, he would threaten to cut off his relationship with her. She believed that it was better to have a relationship no matter how much he mistreated her. Recently, though, she realized that overlooking his mistreatment was harmful to her, and she talked to him about it. He threatened never to talk to her again and accused her of being disrespectful. He ignored her the next three times she came to his house. Finally, he talked to her as if nothing had happened. She felt better, but she knows she'll have to bring it up again.

1 John 4:18 says, "Fear has to do with punishment." God says, "Do not fear the reproach of men or be terrified by their insults" (Isa. 51:7). You're not living up to your values and standards or following your conscience if you're letting the fear of your loved one's reaction direct your steps rather than your faith in God.

Fear of Rejection

The fear of rejection is powerful, but you won't have healthy relationships if you remain afraid to speak the truth, stand up for what you believe, and be who you are. This pattern of behavior may have developed in childhood, especially if you had critical parents or suffered substantial peer rejection.

Doug needed to stop enabling his alcoholic father and drug-addicted brother by providing money. He was afraid because he knew he would be the outcast and rejected by most of his family. It felt overwhelming, but he knew he had to stand up for righteousness.

God does not want us to be afraid of rejection. He wants

us to be strong and capable of standing up for truth. Jesus
gave the disciples this advice regarding rejection: "If anyone
will not welcome you or listen to your words, shake the dust
off your feet when you leave that home or town" (Matt.
10:14). God does not want you bound by the reactions of
other people. He understands, because He suffers pain over
the rejection of His creation, but He does not want you to
be unable to function because of it.

Fear of Change

Even good change is stressful. In difficult relationships
change is even more stressful, because dysfunctional people
often don't have the skills to cope with it. Adjusting to
change requires extra energy, an ability to let go of the results, and flexibility. For a while, change brings a certain level of uncertainty and loss of control, both of which are uncomfortable feelings for people in difficult relationships.
Maybe you fear you can't change. You can. "With God all
things are possible" (Matt. 19:26). Change brings hope. In
order to improve your life and relationships, you have to
risk change.

Donna dreaded telling her daughter that she (Donna)
could no longer care for her children. She feared her
daughter's anger and wondered if she would refuse to bring
the children over. She worried about who would care for
them and knew she would feel responsible if anything bad
happened to them. She knew she didn't have a choice, however, because her health was getting worse, and it was too
much for her.

God can't change you or other people if you desperately
try to keep things the same out of fear. Ps. 112:7 says, "He
will have no fear of bad news; his heart is steadfast, trusting
in the LORD." God's counsel to you is "Have no fear of sudden disaster or of the ruin that overtakes the wicked, for the
LORD will be your confidence and will keep your foot from

being snared" (Prov. 3:25-26). He wants you to do what you know is right and trust Him with the outcome.

Fear of Loss

The things you fear losing most reveal your true priorities. In my difficult relationships, I tended to fear the loss of material possessions, status quo, and convenience more than the loss of more important things, like peace in my home, dignity, self-esteem, respect, and a clear conscience before God. Prov. 15:16-17 says, "Better a little with the fear of the LORD than great wealth with turmoil. Better a meal of vegetables where there is love than a fattened calf with hatred." We're to seek God first (Matt. 6:33), hate evil, and cling to what is good (Rom. 12:9). You need to consider all you're losing and make sure your priorities are right.

Your fears may be realistic, but you can't live today as though what you fear is actually happening—especially since you have no control. Decide to face the loss if and when it happens, because that day may never come. In Matt. 6:25-34, Jesus said not to worry about material things: food, clothes, money, and even our lives. He asked, "Who of you by worrying can add a single hour to his life?" (v. 27).

Some loss may be necessary to make your loved one willing to change. If you fear loss so much that you prevent it at all costs, you may actually be getting in God's way. Many addicts have been miraculously spared injury in an accident that has been their turning point. Others have been injured or injured others and faced the seriousness of their problem from a hospital bed or jail cell. Others face their problems only if they're faced with losing a relationship.

Paul said in Phil. 3:8, "I consider everything a loss compared to the surpassing greatness of knowing Christ Jesus my Lord, for whose sake I have lost all things." Don't let the loss of anything be more important to you than standing for what's right and pleasing to the Lord. Even though it's overwhelming, you can't let the fear of loss keep you from doing what's right.

Fear of Abandonment

Fear of abandonment is an irrational feeling that you'll die emotionally if someone leaves you or threatens to leave you. Any hint of a loss of the relationship or even the security of the relationship causes you to emotionally overreact with anger, panic, insecurity, or fear. You may manifest this in relationships by being clingy, dependent, controlling, or not risking closeness. This fear of abandonment comes from insecurity and unpredictability in your childhood, and it can be a very powerful force underlying your adult relationships. If you know you're from a dysfunctional home and notice that you're having any of these reactions, you have a fear of abandonment. Knowing what you're experiencing helps to minimize the intensity of the feeling, especially when you remind yourself that the feeling is related to past events, not necessarily to what you're dealing with today.

God wants us to be emotionally free of the wounds from our past so that we can have healthy relationships today. The Israelites went to King Rehoboam and asked him to lift the heavy load placed on them from his father (1 Kings 12:4). Go to your Heavenly Father and ask Him to help you remove the yoke of your past by helping you face it and deal with it.

Fear of Being Cut Off

Your difficult loved one may threaten to cut off your relationship when he or she doesn't get his or her way or when you confront issues or make changes. Threats are designed to manipulate you into doing what he or she wants and are rarely followed through, but if they are, you may feel responsible for the break. Remember that it was not your choice. You did what was right and necessary for you, given the circumstances, and your loved one chose to walk away.

Keeping that in mind makes it easier for you to accept the outcome even though it's painful to have someone you care about walk away from you.

Jesus understands what it's like to be deserted (Matt. 26:56). Everyone deserted the apostle Paul, but he realized that God had never deserted him (2 Tim. 4:16-17). God will never forsake you—nothing can separate you from His love (Rom. 8:38-39).

Fear of Intimacy

You may think that you couldn't possibly suffer from fear of intimacy. After all, aren't you spending your life pursuing a close relationship with someone who doesn't seem to want to be close to you? But amazingly, many of the people dealing with difficult relationships suffer from this fear. Being afraid of intimacy means that you're afraid of being vulnerable and known for who you are and unwilling to risk disapproval. You're afraid to allow others to see that you don't have it all together, that you hurt, and that you have moments of weakness and confusion.

Not only was Frances working full-time as a nurse, but she was also raising three daughters, caring for her aged mother, and helping out regularly at church. Everyone admired her abilities and remarked how strong and capable she was. Frances was dying inside. If people only knew how alone and insecure she really felt, they would be shocked. She kept up a good front, though, because she was convinced they would not like her if she revealed how broken and empty she really felt most of the time.

James 5:16 says, "Confess your sins to each other and pray for each other so that you may be healed." God wants you to be honest about your weaknesses except when someone will use the weakness and honesty to hurt you.

Fear of Disappointment

Difficult relationships are filled with unpredictability, unfulfilled expectations, disillusionment, broken promises, and broken dreams. Difficult people are unreliable, moody, unreasonable, irresponsible, and undependable. Difficult people may promise to change, but they don't follow through. They may be sincere at the time or just want to pacify you. Maybe you still jump at any sign of hope that things are getting better and enthusiastically believe whatever you're told. Maybe you remain hopeful without any evidence. Hope is good, but "hope deferred makes the heart sick" (Prov. 13:12). When your loved one makes a promise, you have to accept the possibility of failure to follow through and not let it destroy you.

Addicts and other difficult people who hit bottom are often finally ready to do whatever it takes to stay sober or change. They'll go to a program, get counseling, change their attitudes, and show true repentance. Lasting change comes after hard work, not after simple promises. Yet even then, people sometimes stop growing and slip back into old behaviors. You have to be aware of that risk so you're not devastated.

Your hope must be in God—not a person. When you desire for a specific outcome in any difficult relationship, you have to remember that ultimately your hope is not in that outcome. As David said, "But now, Lord, what do I look for? My hope is in you" (Ps. 39:7).

Fear of Death and Physical Harm

Your loved one may threaten to commit suicide. The threat may be serious or a way to control you through fear.

Every time Joy talked about moving out of the house and getting her own apartment, her mother talked about killing herself, stating that she had nothing to live for. Feeling guilty and afraid, Joy dropped her plans. She later realized that her mother was manipulating her.

If people are truly suicidal, you won't be able to stop them. You're not responsible for anyone's decision to commit suicide. You should try to get help from family, friends, the police, a counselor, or a minister, always remembering that, in the end, that person's choice is beyond your control.

You may also fear the death of your loved one. It could be due to drug and alcohol use, physical health problems, or physically dangerous situations. There's nothing you can do to make someone safe who refuses to do it. You can't make your loved one leave a dangerous environment when he or she wants to stay. Let go of this fear, and trust God with your loved one's life, knowing that God cares but that hearts can be stubborn. You also have to trust Him to carry you through should your fears come to pass.

Perhaps, on the other hand, you fear that you or an innocent person will be harmed physically by someone who is on drugs, is mentally ill, or is abusive. These may be realistic fears that you must do something about. If you or your family members are in danger, you have a responsibility to do what it takes to get protection—even if it feels that you're betraying your loved one.

Fear of Feeling Your Emotions

If you have denied or stuffed your feelings, you may feel overwhelmed when you begin to feel the anger, hurt, and other emotions that are hidden inside you. But if you don't face them, your emotions will rule you without your even knowing it, sabotaging your best intentions. Emotions and unresolved issues continually affect your interpretations, interactions, and relationships. Sometimes your focus on fixing others is to avoid dealing with yourself. Many physical illnesses come from repressed emotions. If you're overwhelmed with the thought of feeling, you may need support to begin to process all you've denied. The feelings will become manageable, and you'll feel more alive and in touch with the real you. Jesus was not afraid to show His emotions; neither was the apostle Paul or King David. God wants us to be real, transparent, and honest. Emotions are a vital part of what God is doing in your life. In Ps. 139, David said God knew everything about him and desired truth in his inner being.

The apostle Paul felt despair over all the trials he endured building the Early Church but concluded that all those things happened to bring him to the place at which he could fully rely on God (2 Cor. 1:8). Feelings have to be felt, but they don't have to control your life.

Some people believe their thoughts and feelings are premonitions. This can be dangerous. I remember a time when I was apprehensive about flying. My friend said to me, "Don't go. I don't feel good about your trip." It unnerved me, but in the end I reasoned that it was her fear and not a sign from God. I went, and the trip was fine.

God speaks through the Bible, people, circumstances, and open doors. It's unwise to give prophetic status to every thought that pops into your head or someone else's.

Fear of What People Will Think

Prov. 29:25 says, "Fear of man will prove to be a snare, but whoever trusts in the LORD is kept safe." You can't live your life afraid of what people will think, or you won't be able to please God or stand by your convictions (Gal. 1:10). You may fear what people will think if you make decisions they disapprove of or they find out the truth about your life. It's not your responsibility to keep everyone happy. As long as you're not intentionally mean and hurtful, let go of their reactions. If people judge you harshly for your problems— that's their issue. There will be those who have not been through anything similar who will make inaccurate judgments. None of us are as empathetic and understanding when we have not been through a particular experience.

Rita was involved in a women's Bible study. She never talked about her personal problems. Her 25-year-old son had schizophrenia. Even though the doctors assured her that she hadn't caused it, she felt people would think she was a failure as a mother. She went through continual problems with him: his refusal to take medication, his psychotic episodes when he heard voices, his arrests and hospitalizations, the fears of his being harmed or harming others.

Rita was preventing herself from being supported by the body of Christ. Not only would she be better off sharing the truth about her life with the women in her Bible study, but she might even be able to help them. As long as you allow the fear of what people might think silence you, you won't be able to get and give the encouragement God has planned for others and you.

Fear of the Unknown

"What if _____?" You fill in the blank. The future is unknown and feels overwhelming and hopeless. You may feel that the only way you can maintain control is to anticipate what's coming and cover your options beforehand by contemplating hundreds of scenarios.

Kim's 35-year-old son was addicted to cocaine. He had been arrested twice, his finances were in shambles, and his wife had left him. Kim was nervous every time the phone rang, but when she didn't hear from him, she imagined all sorts of horrible possibilities: he was dead, hurt in an accident, in jail, or homeless. It was difficult for her to keep her mind on the present and enjoy her other adult children, grandchildren, and retirement with her husband.

Jesus knew this was the tendency of the human race when He told His disciples not to worry about tomorrow (Matt. 6:34). None of us really knows what the next moment may bring, and we should always keep in mind that God's plan may be different than the plans we make (James 4:13-16).

You have real issues to deal with today. Letting your fear of what *might* happen rule your life will result in your losing out on what God has for you today.

WHEN FEAR IS A WARNING

There are times when fear is a warning that should be heeded. Here are some examples of reasonable fears that you should pay attention to: walking in a bad neighborhood at night, falling off a cliff if you get too close to the edge, getting a sexually transmitted disease if your spouse is having sex outside your marriage, your grandchildren being harmed if their parents are severely neglecting them, you or someone else being harmed from someone who gets violent from drugs, anger, or mental illness.

Prov. 22:3 says, "A prudent man sees danger and takes refuge, but the simple keep going and suffer for it." Let some fears lead you to responsible prevention and precautions, or you'll be a simpleminded person who doesn't pay heed to your way and suffers for it.

RESPONDING TO FEAR

Don't Let Fear Win

Consider the following questions when evaluating and analyzing your fears and how they affect your decisions:

- What are you really afraid of?
- Is your fear realistic or unrealistic?
- Is your fear projecting far into the future, or are you actually dealing with it today?
- How does your fear affect your decisions and actions?
- Can you do anything about it right now?
- Are you willing to take necessary action?

Deal with fear by identifying it, feeling it, talking to God and others about it, analyzing how it's affecting your choices, and then say, "So what?" to your fear by doing the right thing anyway. That's the only way to prevent fear from paralyzing and imprisoning you.

Instead of panicking when you feel fearful, refuse to give fear that much power over you. Paul wrote to Timothy,

"God did not give us a spirit of timidity, but a spirit of power, of love and of self-discipline" (2 Tim. 1:7). Self-discipline is translated as a "sound mind" in the King James Version. Paul was telling Timothy to respond to fear with God's strength. Having a sound mind gives you the ability to choose your response to fear. If it's something you're dealing with today, you need the courage to do what you need to do to take care of the situation. If there's nothing you can do, you can respond by trusting God.

Fear is the anticipation that something bad will happen. When it becomes a reality, you stop fearing it and feel other emotions. Job said, "What I feared has come upon me; what I dreaded has happened to me. I have no peace, no quietness; I have no rest, but only turmoil" (Job 3:25-26). At the moment Job's fears came true, he no longer felt fear—instead, he then felt despair, hopelessness, and confusion. You may even have new fears to deal with.

Colette's worst fear was of her son getting in an accident. When it happened, she was surprised at how well she handled it. However, it brought on a new set of fears: "Will he go to jail?" "Will the family judge him harshly?" "Will his girlfriend stay with him?" "Will he lose his job?" "Will he be angry if I refuse to bail him out and pay for a good attorney?" Colette decided to turn all of these new fears over to God. She realized that this might be the thing God used to get Gary to look at his drinking problem. She would handle each problem, with God's help, as it came up.

Dwelling on fear causes anxiety and worry. Reminding yourself that it's just a feeling and not necessarily real helps you put it into a proper perspective.

Trust in the Lord

You trust God by an act of your will, choosing to trust because you know that God is good and trustworthy. God promises to give you strength (Phil. 4:13) and to work all things for your good (Rom. 8:28). That does not mean your way will be easy or that everything will turn out right and no one will suffer. Prov. 3:5-6 says, "Trust in the LORD with all your heart and lean not on your own understanding; in all your ways acknowledge him, and he will make your paths straight."

Once you make a choice to trust, you'll have to exercise self-discipline or soundness of mind by refusing to think anxious thoughts. Phil. 4:6-7 says, "Do not be anxious about anything, but in everything, by prayer and petition, with thanksgiving, present your requests to God. And the peace of God, which transcends all understanding, will guard your hearts and your minds in Christ Jesus." By giving your anxious thoughts and fears to God, you choose to trust rather than let fear rule your life. You'll then experience the peace of God, which comes flooding in when you step out in faith and do what's right.

Ps. 16:8 says, "I have set the LORD always before me. Because he is at my right hand, I will not be shaken." It's a matter of perspective. If you allow your mind to think about God's promises and provision, even though you feel fear, you'll feel more trust. This will enable you to make wiser decisions, because you won't be shaken.

Does that mean everything will work out well for those you love and that those difficult relationships will all be healed? Can God be trusted with your life and the lives of those you love? God says this of wayward Israel:

> *In a desert land he found him, in a barren and howling waste.*
>
> *He shielded him and cared for him; he guarded him as the apple of his eye,*
>
> *Like an eagle that stirs up its nest and hovers over its young,*
> *That spreads its wings to catch them and carries them on its pinions.*
>
> *The LORD alone led him; no foreign god was with him. . . .*

See now that I myself am He! There is no god besides me.

I put to death and I bring to life, I have wounded and I will heal, and no one can deliver out of my hand (Deut. 32:10-12, 39).

You can trust that God!

SPEAK THE TRUTH IN LOVE

Then we will no longer be infants, tossed back and forth by the waves, and blown here and there by every wind of teaching and by the cunning and craftiness of men in their deceitful scheming. Instead, speaking the truth in love, we will in all things grow up into him who is the Head, that is, Christ. —Eph. 4:14-15

P oor communication underlies all difficult relationships. Addictions, dysfunctions, and mental illnesses cloud communication with layers of expectations, resentments, pain, misinterpretations, wrong motives, denial, dishonesty, and blame. Even if your loved one is not able to communicate in a healthy way, *you* need to. Speaking the truth in love is a powerful principle that changes the dynamics of your relationship.

KNOW THE TRUTH

Let Go of Denial

Denial is a very powerful psychological tool that keeps you from facing unpleasant things. It's natural for people to deny that there's a problem until they're ready to face it and address it. Denial can range from mild to extreme. You may temporarily deny your part in a conflict, possibly out of anger or pride, and then later realize you were wrong. It can be so extreme in some cases that a person refuses to admit that a loved one has died.

Denial is different than lying. Lying is a deliberate deception for the purpose of covering up something you know is true. Denial is a protective filter that you put over your life to keep you from facing things you're not able to deal with; the downside is that it prevents you from using the truth to make wise decisions. Again, Prov. 22:3 says, "A prudent man sees danger and takes refuge, but the simple keep going and suffer for it."

Some church doctrines encourage denial. "Faith teaching" says that you should refuse to accept reality and instead speak the truth into being. This teaching would tell you to believe that your relationship is healed, your loved one is well, your problems are gone, and your bank account is full. It tells you to ignore reality and to speak and believe into existence whatever you want. God has not given you the power to cause things to happen with your words or with your faith. You don't have to live in fear that you're preventing healing by saying what's real. It's not wrong to say that you or your loved one is hurting, sick, poor, or struggling with a severe problem. God honors truth. Prov. 12:22 says, "The LORD detests lying lips, but he delights in men who are truthful." Jesus said truth produces freedom (John 8:32). He does not want us to pretend.

You'll likely go through four stages before you can come to terms in a healthy way with difficult circumstances, people, and events: denial, blame and anger, sadness and grief, and acceptance.

Denial comes first as a sort of shock absorber. Until you can absorb the impact of the situation, denial takes the bumps and dips. When you can finally begin to admit the truth about your loved one's problem, you may feel anger toward God, yourself, others, and your troubled loved one. Eventually the anger you feel will turn to a deep sadness, and you'll grieve the loss of the things you want but don't have, including the loss of your dreams and hopes. When the grief subsides, you arrive at a place of peaceful acceptance where you can face the reality of the situation and make necessary decisions.

Ruth knew that John wasn't an easy child but believed he was just a restless boy. Her husband didn't even seem to notice that John was a problem. Over the years, Ruth gradually realized that John's problems were increasing. She finally took him to a psychologist, who diagnosed him with a learning disability and attention deficit disorder. As a teenager, John became unmanageable. His drug use escalated to a cocaine addiction at age 23. Her husband continues to deny that John had any problems. He also minimizes John's drug addiction, saying lots of young adults try it for a while. Ruth doesn't know which hurts and angers her more—her husband's refusal to admit the truth or John's drug use and problems. She has tried everything to get both of them to face the truth and fix things. Neither wants to listen. She finds herself blaming her husband for John's problems, then God, herself, and John. Then she slips into a depression, feeling the hopelessness of the situation. Eventually she will come to a place of acceptance and decide how she can best deal with both her husband and John.

As you come to a place of facing the truth about your life and the people you love, you may find others have difficulty hearing you; they deny your truth, defend themselves, and refuse to consider what you have to say. On the other hand, your willingness to state the truth may set them on a path of discovering that truth for themselves.

Let Go of Self-Doubt

You must learn to trust yourself. Having others disagree with you doesn't automatically make you wrong. Verbal and emotional abuse and dysfunctional communication can take a tremendous amount of energy to counter, but you can hold to your perceptions if you realize that what other people say is the result of the dysfunction or may not be from pure motives. Some people want to tell lies, cover up, manipulate, and control, so they deliberately attack and

mislead you. "He who winks with his eye is plotting perversi-
ty; he who purses his lips is bent on evil" (Prov. 16:30). As
much as you don't want to admit it, your loved one may
choose to deceive.

You may feel confused over what you see and hear. Your
loved one is telling you the opposite of what you see, telling
you that he or she is clean—yet you see signs of drug use.
She tells you her marriage is better, but you see her husband continue to treat her abusively. He tells you he's working, but you haven't seen a paycheck. She promises change,
but does nothing to change. You need to watch actions to
see if they're consistent with words. If they don't match, you
need to recognize that words are empty promises.

Knowing the truth means facing the facts about your life:
Your loved one has a serious problem. You're affected by it,
feeling scared, worried, angry, embarrassed, depressed, disappointed, guilty, confused, and compassionate at the same
time. You haven't been able to fix it. You wonder what God
expects. You're tired of struggling, pretending, and holding
everything together.

The most common emotion you'll feel is anger. If you
don't feel anger, you may be keeping the peace at any cost.
Anger is a necessary emotion and should be felt when encountering wrong. Jesus got angry when people were disre-
specting God's Temple by selling sacrifices in it, becoming
so angry that He even threw their tables over (John 2:15).

On the other hand, if all you feel is anger, it's masking
other emotions. Anger is easy to feel, gives you energy, and
allows you to feel powerful and in control for a while. Un-
derneath the anger you may be feeling fear, sadness, hurt,
disappointment, fear, or guilt. Try to feel all your emotions.
It's important to understand the truth about what you're
feeling in order to effectively communicate it.

You'll have to give yourself time to clarify your truth.
When you feel confused, it's helpful to write about it or talk

to someone you can trust. Eventually, you'll begin to trust your feelings and perceptions. You'll come to see that many of your intuitions were right from the start. As the truth becomes clear, you'll begin to be empowered to make changes in your own life and in the way you relate to your loved ones.

SPEAK THE TRUTH

Be Willing to Confront

Jesus confronted people in a very direct way, always speaking the truth (John 1:17). You have heard people say, "Be accepting, loving, and kind like Jesus." They're inferring passivity and tolerance. In reality, Jesus was hard-hitting and cutting with His remarks, especially when He felt someone was manipulating Him, tricking Him, or was against Him. He was quick to point out hypocrisy and lies. Consider these remarks of His to the Pharisees: "You brood of vipers, how can you who are evil say anything good? For out of the overflow of the heart the mouth speaks" (Matt. 12:34). "Woe to you, teachers of the law and Pharisees, you hypocrites!" (Matt. 23:29). "You snakes! You brood of vipers! How will you escape being condemned to hell?" (Matt. 23:33). And this comment to the Sadducees: "You are in error because you do not know the Scriptures or the power of God" (Matt. 22:29). And these to the disciples: "Are you still so dull?" (Matt. 15:16). "You of little faith, why are you talking among yourselves about having no bread? Do you still not understand?" (Matt. 16:8-9). "Could you men not keep watch with me for one hour?" (Matt. 26:40).

Approaching your difficult loved one in a loving way lets him or her know you're holding him or her accountable because of your commitment to the relationship, his or her well-being, and to what's pure. Tough love says, "I love you enough to be willing to cause you discomfort or pain, in the hopes of helping you better your life and mine by not continuing to do these destructive things." Although you can't force change or even agreement, you're responsible for presenting the truth. There are times you must "answer a fool according to his folly, or he will be wise in his own eyes" (Prov. 26:5).

You'll need to confront when your loved one's behavior is destructive to himself or herself, you, or others. "Encourage one another daily, as long as it is called Today, so that none of you may be hardened by sin's deceitfulness" (Heb. 3:13). Confrontation is sometimes necessary, but there are ways to do it to maximize its effectiveness.

Be Honest

When you want to speak the truth in love to your loved one, you'll have to begin by being honest about yourself. You may be surprised to learn that you've contributed to the poor intimacy and communication. Out of fear you may have held back the truth about how you've felt about many things, not only about your loved one's problems but also your weaknesses, sins, fears, and struggles. A deep level of honesty may be uncomfortable and new for you. You may not have paid attention to what you were feeling and thinking since you were so focused on changing your loved one. Regardless of the reasons for your lack of honesty and openness, you need to take a risk by being vulnerable about who you are and how you feel. The risk involves the possibility of rejection, ridicule, conflict, disapproval, and anger. But not being honest prevents your relationship from growing deeper and your loved one from knowing the truth about you. You can't have intimacy without truth. Speaking the truth gives your loved one the opportunity to see what's happening now rather than waiting until things deteriorate further. The Lord wants you to speak the truth from your heart (Ps. 15:2).

You'll need to be honest about your feelings, thoughts, needs, weaknesses, and fears. You need to share how your loved one's struggles are affecting you as well as what you see. The focus is not on trying to force him or her to agree with you. You're expressing your thoughts and perceptions, taking full responsibility for how you're feeling and reacting. When you present your concerns in this way, you'll find that your loved one is less likely to be defensive.

Be Direct

Try to be as direct as possible. Direct and straightforward communication is powerful. Dysfunctional communication is indirect and unclear, with the expectation for others to decipher its meaning. One of the purposes of being truthful is for you to take responsibility for what you see, feel, think, need, and do. Indirect communication avoids responsibility by shifting it to the other person, expecting him or her to guess at what you mean. It often causes more conflict and confusion. Direct communication lets everyone know exactly where you stand.

Direct communication also allows you to say what you need to say in as few words as possible. I often gave long lectures to my loved ones with the goal of helping them to understand. The more desperate I got for them to "get it," the more intense I got. I later learned that I could make my point much more powerfully using just a few words rather than a lecture they resented and tuned out.

Here are some examples of short, direct statements. Feel the power in them compared to an emotional, argumentative lecture: "I'm very worried about you." "I feel belittled when you put me down." "I'm uncomfortable around you when you're drinking." "I feel angry when I see Jack treat you badly." "I'm concerned about our relationship. I want to be closer to you." "I'm having difficulty with your moods. I don't know if I can continue to deal with them if you don't get help." "I'm frustrated that we can't reach an understanding." "I don't want you to bring drugs into this house.

If you do, you'll have to move out." "I feel as if your struggles are a reflection on me. I feel like I was a failure as a parent." "I don't know how much longer I can hold on to our marriage if it doesn't improve."

Clear statements say what you need to say. They don't threaten, intimidate, manipulate, or control. They don't require agreement. They're more difficult to argue with, because they simply state your position. Think before you speak, and say only what you really mean in as few words as possible.

Be Accurate

Accuracy is important. Stick to the specific facts rather than general accusations. You don't want to assume that the other person knows what you're talking about or accuse based on incomplete information. You may think that you don't do that, but in reality you do it all the time. It has to do with assumptions.

An assumption is something you automatically believe to be true—without proof. It requires an interpretation—yours. You assume causes. For instance, if you see your loved one looking sad, you may assume you know why he or she is sad. Or you assume that his or her anger is due to something you did—when it may be related to something entirely different. You assume intentions when you believe someone didn't call you because he or she doesn't care; or that he or she didn't go to work because of getting drunk. Intentions have to do with the reason people do what they do. You also assume people's feelings. Ever told your loved one how he or she feels? Ever argued about the feelings he or she is expressing, implying that his or her feelings and interpretations are wrong? You've said things like "You shouldn't feel that way." "That's silly." "I know you're hurt."

When you speak the truth in love, you want to be careful not to assume. Instead, approach the matter as if you want to search out an abandoned mine. Go cautiously, carefully, questioning, and exploring. Whenever you see behavior or information that triggers a judgment—*stop*. Ask your loved one for clarification before assuming. Give him or her the opportunity to explain. Or maybe he or she will choose not to explain —then you have to back off, respecting boundaries.

Be Respectful

Nonverbal body language and tone of voice are often more important than what you say. It's very likely that yours have communicated contempt and disrespect for your loved one in subtle and obvious ways. Speaking the truth without love can be destructive.

Respect comes from the awareness that God has given each person the right to make personal choices. You have to keep that in mind as you approach your loved one so that you don't unconsciously treat him or her with contempt. Your adult child was only a loan from God. You were entrusted with guiding and disciplining a young child, but not an adult child. The relationship and responsibility changed at adulthood. Similarly, your parents don't have to answer to you about their behavior. No adult needs your approval to make a choice. Be sure your tone of voice and body language communicate respect for this autonomy.

Respect also means you speak to your loved one with kindness. Kindness makes your words easier to hear and insures you'll feel good about what you said. "As God's chosen people, holy and dearly loved, clothe yourselves with compassion, kindness, humility, gentleness and patience" (Col. 3:12). "When the kindness and love of God our Savior appeared, he saved us, not because of righteous things we had done, but because of his mercy" (Titus 3:4-5). The apostle Peter told Christians to add love to their brotherly kindness (2 Pet. 1:7). Kindness precedes love. In order for your loved one to receive your truth in a spirit of love, it has to come from a spirit of kindness, respect, and consideration for his or her circumstances and humanity. Your loved one is probably already suffering from low self-esteem, insecurity, and feelings of self-reproach. The most angry and mean people are often covering deep wounds and insecurities, hurting others because of their pain. If you want your loved one to make improvements, don't treat him or her as though the situation is hopeless and he or she is worthless. Treating even the lowliest with esteem communicates love, giving an incentive to improve, rather than reinforcing feelings of failure. That's what Jesus would do if He were communicating your message.

Be Humble

Being humble means that you keep a proper perspective on who you are in relation to God and others. All of us have problems; none of us is perfect. You cannot approach your loved one with an arrogant and self-righteous attitude. You are not, in the eyes of God, any more valuable or righteous than he or she, even if you don't do the same things. Anytime you reprove others for their faults, you must do it with gentleness. As Gal. 6:1 says, "Brothers, if someone is caught in a sin, you who are spiritual should restore him gently" because you are aware that "you may also be tempted."

Humility also means that you're willing to admit when you're wrong. Audrey said, "I was as defensive as my daughter. I wouldn't let her point out my faults any more than she let me address hers. I didn't realize that I was doing the same thing I was accusing her of doing. Our conversations changed when I stopped being defensive. She began to feel safe admitting her faults, too, after a while."

God wants us to focus on our own shortcomings before we focus on the shortcomings of others (Matt. 7:1-2). When you're speaking the truth in love, you have to be careful that you don't display arrogance or self-righteousness. Both of these indicate that you feel superior to your loved one. Instead, "clothe [yourself] with humility toward one another" (1 Pet. 5:5). Humility prepares the way for your words to be received.

Be Persistent

Be persistent in speaking your truth. You can't expect instant change or even a positive reaction. The reality is that speaking the truth may produce new conflict in your relationship. It will force you and your loved one to deal with things you've both ignored. He or she may react with fear, insecurity, resistance, anger, ridicule, hurt, and increased control due to the inability to handle what you have to say. That's OK. Let him or her have feelings and reactions—then detach. Emily told her father how his negative comments hurt her. He laughed and told her she was too sensitive. She refused to react with anger but continued to tell him how she felt. Larry told his wife he did not want her to ridicule him in front of the children. She denied that she was doing it, but Larry continued to point it out when it happened.

Additionally, it's good for you to say what you need to say and know that you've communicated your truth. Eventually you'll be able to decide if you need to follow your words with an action or consequence. Unless you've persistently said your truth, you'll probably be unable to do that. You may have trained your loved one not to listen by empty threats, passivity, and angry emotional outbursts in the past. He or she may know that as long as you're venting, you won't follow up with action. Change the way you communicate, and follow with action. If your actions change along with your words, you'll be communicating your truth effectively.

Be Open-minded

When you speak the truth, your loved one may begin to communicate more honestly too. Some of that truth may be hard for you to take. Pain from the past may be brought up, old resentments, hurts, and memories that you may not want to deal with. No matter how hard it is for you to hear it, you need to listen. It's particularly difficult to listen when you come with something you need to express, and the conversation shifts to his or her issue. Rather than your being the initiator or speaker in control, you now become the listener. Resist the temptation to force the conversation back to your issue. If your goal is to have a relationship based on truth, you need to be able to hear your loved one's truth too.

Listening is a skill. Good listeners put their own agenda completely aside mentally, emotionally, and verbally and focus completely on what the speaker has to say. Anger expressed in this context may be healthy, because anger needs to be discussed in order to dispel it. Resist the urge to counter, argue, agree, disagree, add, fix, lecture, or take away from what's being said. Instead, simply acknowledge and repeat what you hear. The goal becomes understanding exactly what your loved one is feeling, thinking, and perceiving. Listening can be particularly difficult when you disagree with what is being said or when it's being said about you and it's triggering fears, insecurities, guilt, anger, sadness, and other emotions. But you have to do it anyway. When your loved one feels heard and understood, he or she will be better able to hear you. Healing starts with exposing the hidden thoughts and feelings.

Be Reasonable

In a difficult relationship it's easy to overreact instantaneously to things and exaggerate their importance. Remember that some of the problems and irritations you experience are part of normal living. Forgetfulness, misunderstandings, hurt feelings, sickness, differences of opinions, mistakes, irritations, quirks, and bad moods are a part of everyone's life. You have to keep a proper perspective.

Some of the things about your loved one that annoy you

are just idiosyncrasies and personality differences that everyone has. The difficulty lies in assigning a degree of importance to the many problems and irritations you encounter each day. Try to overlook things that aren't big deals.

One way to help you figure out if it's a big deal or a little deal is to ask yourself, *How important is it? Is it life threatening? Is it immoral? Is it something that affects me in the long term? Is it harmful to me or others? What are the ramifications? How would it affect me to let it go? How will it affect me to say something about it? Is it worth mentioning, or will that cause more problems? Is it something I'll remember or will easily forget? What's my state of mind at the moment? Could it be that I'm tired and that things are therefore appearing to be more serious than they are? Am I reacting to what's happening now, or am I angry about the past?*

The balance to speaking the truth in love is learning that there are times that "love covers a multitude of sins" (1 Pet. 4:8) and "is not easily angered" (1 Cor. 13:5). Those are the times to overlook small things.

Be Discerning

"Even a fool is thought wise if he keeps silent, and discerning if he holds his tongue" (Prov. 17:28). There are times when it's wise not to say anything at all. "Do not answer a fool according to his folly, or you will be like him yourself" (Prov. 26:4). The secret is knowing when to speak and when to keep quiet. There will be times when you know your words will only provoke anger, an argument, or an irrational response. That's the time to be silent. Speaking the truth in love is a lofty goal, but realistically, there will be times when you can't do it.

Also be quiet when your words will be destructive and angry. These are the times when answering irrational accusations and comments would provoke you to answer irrationally or when you're volatile and emotional.

Don't try to talk to someone who's under the influence of drugs or alcohol, raging, mentally unstable, or completely unreasonable. It's useless and can be dangerous. If you're dealing with physical violence, use wisdom. Taking care of yourself comes before everything else.

Knowing when to answer and when to keep quiet requires you to know yourself, know your loved one, and to have the self-restraint to hold your tongue.

Finally, present a little truth at a time rather than dumping all of it onto your loved one at once. He or she will probably be more receptive if given small portions easily digestible rather than being stuffed with all your unexpressed truth. Above all, expressing your truth in love is the goal, not forcing your loved one to agree with you or do what you want.

FORGIVE

Bear with each other and forgive whatever grievances you may have against one another. Forgive as the Lord forgave you. —Col. 3:13

Y ou may or may not be aware of your need to forgive your loved one. You may be so consumed with worry and concern right now that you think you're not resentful. Yet realistically, there's a strong possibility that there's at least some anger and resentment in your heart related to your loved one's problem. Or maybe amidst all your other emotions you're aware of your deep-seated anger and resentment. After all, you are convinced that *if he or she would change, the problems would be solved.*

There may be others you feel resentment toward. Perhaps there are people in your life who don't support your concerns or efforts to help your loved one. Perhaps someone did things in the past or is doing things today that you believe hurt your loved one and make the problem worse. Others may be angry with you because of the choices you've made regarding your loved one, and you may be resentful regarding the disapproval.

You may even blame yourself for past mistakes and for the inability to fix the problem today.

Forgiveness involves canceling a debt, pardoning an offense, or letting go of resentments. Conversely, being unforgiving means holding someone accountable for the debt or offense, holding on to one's right to receive his or her just payment in whatever manner he or she feels would release the debt.

Heb. 12:15 warns that a root of bitterness could spill over

into all your relationships, poisoning them with your negative feelings and anger, causing problems in all areas of your life. The seeds of anger and hurt fertilized by blame and judgment produce hatred. Hatred is an intense feeling borne out of wounded love, thwarted desire, and deep hurt. It's not the absence of feeling.

A lack of forgiveness affects not only you and your loved one but innocent bystanders as well, causing you to mistreat others. Anger and resentment can turn into depression and anxiety and cause physical illnesses. Bitterness poisons your outlook on life, making you negative, cynical, and distrustful of other people.

A lack of forgiveness affects all aspects of your relationship with your loved one. When you refuse to forgive, your heart is at least partially hard and closed. You actually view your loved one as if he or she is disadvantaged, inferior to you, needing to offer a payback, even if it's just an apology or acknowledgment of wrong. You may be unwilling to look at your personal faults in the relationship, instead thinking, *I'll look at myself when he apologizes to me,* or *She owes me for what she did to me first,* thereby refusing to take responsibility for your own actions and excusing them. You may be overly sensitive, since stored resentments are experienced as an open wound. Future actions and words may be misinterpreted or overreacted to, causing even more misunderstanding and confusion in the relationship.

Your loved one may be aware of your resentment and as a result be afraid to be honest or ask for his or her needs to be met due to the unpaid debt held; or he or she may defensively respond with resentment toward you. Resentments build layer upon layer of misunderstanding. It's common for both to feel misunderstood, hurt, and taken advantage of. After all, your loved one has his or her perspective regarding the situation and may view you differently than you see yourself. An unforgiving heart places a wall between you and your loved one. Until it's removed, the relationship is not able to heal, and you and your loved one are unable to deal with current issues openly in a mutually respectful way.

Conversely, forgiveness opens the door for healing both within you and your loved one. It gives the relationship a new beginning and allows both parties to negotiate and communicate from an equal position. Both you and your loved one will feel a release when forgiveness is offered. Both can then let go of the offense and move forward.

WHAT FORGIVENESS IS NOT

Forgiveness Is Not Forgetting

Forgiveness does not mean you have to forget. You have no control over the recording of events in your mind or when those memories and feelings surface. You have control only over what you do with them once they come up.

It's not easy to forget the pain, agony, nights of tears, waste of time, money and potential, fears, lies, hurt, anger, and embarrassment. But even if you would like to erase all of it from your mind, you can't. Maybe God doesn't want you to.

It's important that you know where you came from to appreciate where you are now. God wanted the Israelites to remember that they were slaves in Egypt and that He brought them out of captivity (Deut. 5:15). You need to remember so you can understand how your past affects who you are today and how unresolved needs and past experiences shape your interactions and reactions. Forgiveness requires that you know how you were affected by the events you resent.

Time helps by minimizing the vividness of most memories and pain, which gives you a natural detachment, as long as you don't purposefully dredge them up again. "Resent" means "to feel again." You can allow yourself to wallow in a memory, feeling sorry for yourself, thinking about the injustice, the injury, the pain, and the consequences, mulling it over from every angle until you're lost in the memory, reliving every aspect.

Or you can remember it and choose to do something different with it. Instead of mulling it over, you can recommit to forgive and to view the event in the light of God's grace, healing, provision, and restoration, rejoicing in His faithfulness to you.

Forgiveness Is Not Excusing or Condoning

God forgives us and yet clearly disapproves of our sin. This is the spirit of forgiveness He wants us to have for our loved ones.

It's not inconsistent to follow through with consequences even though forgiveness is offered. In 2 Sam. 11—18, God did this with King David when he committed adultery and murder. Parents do this when they punish misbehavior but continue to love their child. God established the law of reaping and sowing; those who sin will reap destruction, and those that sow in the Spirit will reap eternal life (Gal. 6:7-9).

Forgiveness means that you're taking care of yourself by letting go of the right to avenge or demand repayment of the wrong. It's in no way excusing the wrong that was done.

Forgiveness Is Not Dependent on Repentance

Can you forgive without your loved one being sorry or even realizing that he or she was wrong? While on the Cross, Jesus prayed, "Father, forgive them, for they do not know what they are doing" (Luke 23:34). Jesus asked God to forgive when the people's hearts were hard. They were sneering, casting lots for his clothing, and mocking Him (Luke 23:34-39). Not only were they not seeking forgiveness or admitting they were wrong—they were rejoicing in His crucifixion. The act of forgiveness is unrelated to the person's request. Yet restoration of relationship is done only when both show a desire for it, as one of the thieves dying with Jesus did (Luke 23:40-41).

You can forgive completely without any admission or awareness of wrongdoing by the person you're forgiving, but you don't have to resume the relationship.

Forgiveness Is Not Reconciliation

Forgiveness can occur without reconciliation, but reconciliation cannot occur without forgiveness. Forgiveness requires one person; reconciliation requires two. Reconciliation involves the agreement of you and your loved one to actively pursue a restored relationship.

In fact, at times it may be unhealthy to reconcile with a loved one who has not acknowledged the wrong and repented of it. Forgiveness does not involve being a doormat and allowing others to continue to abuse or mistreat you.

The Bible places a great deal of emphasis on reconciliation. Rom. 12:18, quoted previously, says, "If it is possible, as far as it depends on you, live at peace with everyone." Jesus told his disciples that if they were praying and remembered that someone was upset with them, they were to stop praying, go to their brother to be reconciled, and then return to pray (Matt. 5:23-24). Paul repeatedly told the Christians to live in a spirit of unity (Rom. 15:5; Eph. 4:3). Yet Paul also suggested that a broken relationship might be used by God to bring a brother to repentance (1 Cor. 5:1-5). There's a time to reconcile and a time to be estranged, but forgiveness is offered in both.

Forgiveness Is Not Weakness

It takes a stronger character to forgive than to hold a grudge. Human nature naturally resents and seeks retaliation. Even small children instinctively hit back when hurt by others. It's part of our survival instinct to protect ourselves, yet God wants to turn that weakness into strength through the taking on of His nature (1 Cor. 1:27), in which we learn compassion, kindness, and forgiveness (Eph. 4:32).

It's through the power of not taking revenge and loving your enemies that you fulfill the higher law of love that Jesus talked about in the Sermon on the Mount (Matt. 5:43-48). Rom. 12:17-21 says that when you give up your right to seek revenge, you allow God to deal with your loved one, but when you take revenge, you make your anger and resentment the force. It doesn't work. God has asked you to fight evil by overcoming it with good. Part of that good is forgiveness instead of payback.

If others perceive your forgiveness as weakness, there's nothing you can do except continue to take care of yourself. Forgiveness doesn't stop you from taking steps to prevent being hurt again. It's entirely appropriate to follow through with consequences, even though you forgive. God allows us to suffer consequences even though He forgives us. Your distrust, emotional distance, and protective decisions are the result of your loved one's choices and are part of his or her consequences. If you have been lied to, it's reasonable for you to distrust and set up appropriate safeguards for yourself. If he or she has gotten sober for short periods of time before, it's legitimate for you to wait for a longer track record. If your parent has mistreated you all your life and finally apologizes, it's natural for you to be distanced and cautious for a while.

Forgiveness Is Not Denial

Denial involves the refusal to admit the truth. In reality, you can't truly forgive unless you first admit the truth about the offense you're forgiving. Forgiveness is really coming to terms with the offense and the offender. You may not want to, but you have to grieve the losses you experienced, feel the pain, feel the anger, and then come to the place at which you accept that there's nothing you can do to change it. Not feeling the emotions and pain may be repression, which is emotionally unhealthy. Minimizing or rationalizing the event is also unhealthy, because your forgiveness then is not predicated on truth. You would then be forgiving a lesser or different offense.

You have to deal with the past in whatever way you need to so that it doesn't hinder you in doing everything you need to do today (Heb. 12:1). Sometimes the only way you can throw off the past is by remembering it enough to forgive.

Forgiveness Is Not Superiority

True forgiveness is motivated by compassion, empathy, humility, and mercy, the opposite of a spirit of superiority or self-grandiosity. Remembering that you're also imperfect and in need of forgiveness from God and others keeps you from feeling superior (Gal. 6:1).

If you hold your forgiveness over your loved one's head, saying in effect, "Look how much I forgave you," then you have not offered true forgiveness, because true forgiveness erases the need for payback, gratitude, or acknowledgment.

What Forgiveness Is

Forgiveness Is a Choice

Your loved one can't demand forgiveness from you. Forgiveness has to be given voluntarily in order to be real. It's often a choice that first involves a willingness to forgive. Sometimes you have to ask God for the willingness to be made willing. You may not feel like forgiving, but you can start the process with a desire.

If you're having trouble forgiving, you can pray for the person, asking God to bless him or her. Jesus said, "Pray for those who persecute you" (Matt. 5:44). That prayer will often change the hardness of your heart.

Forgiveness is not a feeling but a decision of the will—although you'll feel many things, including joy and a sense of relief, when you make the decision to forgive.

Forgiveness Is Letting Go of Revenge

Forgiveness is granting the offender a release from the obligation to repay a debt. This feeling of indebtedness for mistakes is part of our nature. We readily feel obligated to apologize, saying, "I owe you an apology." We also feel entitled to an apology or retribution when others offend us.

Jesus set the standard. You are to love your enemy rather than seek revenge (Matt. 5:43-44). Revenge requires judgment, the carrying-out of a sentence that you have decided your loved one deserves. You're not the Righteous Judge; you're not able to judge fairly and purely. Rejoicing in the downfall of those who hurt you requires that you judge them first. Jesus warned in Matt. 7:1-2 not to judge or condemn. This does not mean you can't evaluate wrong behavior but rather that you can't condemn people, since it's only by God's grace that you're saved in the first place.

Retaliation leads to more violence and injury. Repaying a wrong with a wrong leaves that wrong unatoned for, continuing a vicious cycle of hate and injury.

Forgiveness Is Unlimited

If forgiveness is limited to a finite number of times, then it's not genuine forgiveness. God does not set a limit on the number of times He'll forgive you. He does not remember your previous sins and is therefore not keeping track (Ps. 103:12). Love "keeps no record of wrongs" (1 Cor. 13:5), so it can't count. When Peter asked Jesus if he could stop forgiving after seven times, Jesus told him that forgiveness is without a number (Matt. 18:21). Jesus was stating that forgiveness should be a continual part of your life. If you keep count of how many times you forgive, it means that you're holding on to the deed, as if forgiveness had never occurred.

Forgiveness Is Reciprocal

You forgive because God forgives you (Col. 3:13). The more you've been forgiven, the easier it is for you to forgive others. If you find you have difficulty forgiving, it may be because you've been judged harshly. The most judgmental people are often those who have been brutally criticized from childhood and are extremely hard on themselves. If this describes you, you need to start with forgiving yourself and accepting your own imperfections.

When you offer forgiveness to your loved one, he or she may apologize. That will be a relief for you and may begin reconciliation. However, there's no guarantee that it will happen. Your forgiveness is totally unrelated to an apology.

Forgiveness Is a Process

Forgiveness is not a single act, nor is it easy to do, especially for big issues: divorce, adultery, addictions, abuse, death, abandonment, and criminal acts. Different personalities have varying propensities toward forgiveness and resentment. Life experiences (especially childhood) also affect how you forgive as you learned how to handle emotions and relationships from watching and interacting with others. Nevertheless, forgiveness is a process for everyone.

Forgiveness may have to be done slowly. You will have to first come to terms with the widespread effects of the offense over time, especially for traumatic issues.

Forgiving too soon may actually be unhealthy and a sign that the process was not truthful. Instead, it may mean that you're merely stating empty words or saying what you believe you have to say. True forgiveness takes forethought, time, and anguish.

FORGIVE YOURSELF

You may actually have more difficulty forgiving yourself than others.

Saul murdered Christians, yet God redeemed him, changed his name to Paul, and used him mightily for His kingdom. God never reminded him of his past. Paul let go of his past by living for God in the present (Acts 9:1-9; Gal. 1:13).

You're using the hindsight and strength you have today and applying it to your past. You did not know what you know now back then; if you did know it, you were not able to do things differently for some reason.

It's OK to feel guilt about things you've done wrong. The purpose of guilt is to let you know you made a mistake so that you'll repent (2 Cor. 7:10). David said, "My guilt has overwhelmed me like a burden too heavy to bear" (Ps. 38:4). The Holy Spirit works through your conscience to convict you of sin. If you're not being convicted, something's wrong.

On the other hand, if you feel guilty about everything, you'll have more difficulty discerning which feelings are convictions from the Holy Spirit versus your overly critical conscience.

Shame is different than guilt. Shame tells you that you're bad and worthless. It comes from living in dysfunctional families and not being loved unconditionally. When you feel that you're a mistake, a loser, no good, and incapable of doing anything right, recognize this as shame. God doesn't want you to feel shame. He let His Son die for you on the Cross. That act testifies to the fact that you're valuable in His eyes and worthy of being redeemed. Allow yourself to admit your mistakes—without feeling that you're a mistake.

Try to accept that you did the best you could at the time. "God's kindness leads you toward repentance" (Rom. 2:4), not His harsh judgment. Since God forgives you—forgive yourself.

Honest reflection and an acceptance of your mistakes are important, but understanding why you did what you did helps you to have grace and mercy toward yourself—the same grace and mercy God has toward you and wants you to extend toward others.

You can forgive yourself by doing the following:

- Acknowledge your mistakes.
- Believe you did the best you could at the time.
- Look for the good in your past.
- Accept the fact that you can't change the past.
- Accept God's forgiveness.
- Forgive yourself.
- Make changes in your life today so you don't repeat the mistakes.
- Expect God to redeem your past and use it for His glory.
- Look for ways to comfort and encourage others with the things you've learned.
- Expect God to work in your loved one's life as He has worked in yours.

The Christian life is a growth process. God doesn't start with perfect people. He redeems and uses imperfect people. Treat yourself the way you would treat a friend if he or she came to you and told you your story. What would you say? Would you offer compassion and mercy as Jesus would do, or would you offer the harsh judgment you often extend toward yourself?

RESULTS OF FORGIVENESS

Resentment and bitterness cause physical health problems, anxiety, poor self-esteem, depression, destructive relationships, a blocked relationship with God, less productivity, decreased enjoyment of life, and generational pain and destruction. Forgiveness results in spiritual and psychological healing, reconciliation, a closer relationship with God, improved physical health, and inner peace.

Why forgive? Rich Buhler in his book *Pain and Pretending*

(Nashville: Thomas Nelson Publishers, 1991, 197-98) gives the following reasons: Jesus says to. It aids your own recovery. It releases the person's power over you.

Forgiveness is a gift you give not only to your loved one but also to yourself. The gift is freedom—freedom from being chained to the weight of the past so you can live fully today, and freedom for your loved one by the offering of a new start and a glimpse of God's grace and mercy.

SET BOUNDARIES

God did not give us a spirit of timidity, but a spirit of power, of love and of self-discipline. —2 Tim. 1:7

Y ou will give an account of your life to God—not your loved one's life. Consequently, it is up to you to live your life, making wise choices not only in how you use the material resources God gave you but also in what you do with your time and influence. You are actually Christ's ambassador, fulfilling the ministry of reconciliation, representing Christ "as though God were making his appeal through [you]" (2 Cor. 5:20). Therefore, everything you do should parallel what Christ would do in your circumstances. You're not only responsible for controlling your actions but are also interacting in your relationships in ways that bring people closer to God. Some people will choose darkness over light (John 3:19), maybe even your loved one, at least for the time being. You can be light in that darkness by setting a standard both through your example and your limits.

Jesus demonstrated boundaries in His interactions with people. He chose when and how to respond, always in full control of himself and what He allowed others to do to Him. He willingly went to the Cross at the appointed time, but withdrew himself from dangerous situations before that. He held people responsible for their actions while consistently demonstrating authority and integrity (Mark 1:22; Luke 4:32), all the while demonstrating a love that enabled Him to die on the Cross.

Your boundaries may differ from your loved ones' preferences, choices, and wants. They may even cause conflict in your relationship. Jesus warned that following Him would cause family divisions (Matt. 10:34-36). It's not God's first choice that any relationship have a breach, but it may result from making a stand for the higher good of following Christ and standing for righteousness.

WEAK BOUNDARIES

Even people with strong boundaries find those boundaries weakened by association with abuse, addictions, and dysfunction in relationships. It takes a significant amount of strength, vigilance, and self-respect to maintain boundaries when they're constantly assaulted and tested. It takes effort to decide what to do amidst the emotional turmoil of difficult relationships.

If your loved one does not want to be accountable for his or her actions, he or she may act in ways that purposefully challenge and undermine your right to set limits. "A mocker resents correction" (Prov. 15:12), and "a fool finds pleasure in evil conduct" (Prov. 10:23). Boundaries challenge your loved one's control of you. You have not only the right but also the responsibility to set boundaries. Expect him or her to be upset and angry, threaten, test your limits, and accuse you of abandonment and being mean. Expect resistance and an attempt to push you back toward your enabling behavior. It won't last forever. One of the reasons you've been afraid to set limits is because you feel uncomfortable, guilty, or fearful of this negative reaction. When you're aware of it beforehand, you'll be less likely to back down.

Following through with consequences when your boundaries are violated takes strength. You may struggle with boundaries for any or all of the following reasons:

- You don't trust your thoughts, feelings, and perceptions.
- You would rather give in to keep the peace.

- You think being a good Christian means you shouldn't cause people pain.
- You're waiting for God to change your loved one.
- You believe you should submit and give up your rights.
- You're afraid of your loved one's reaction.
- You know your boundaries will not be respected anyway.
- You can't stand seeing your loved one suffer.

As difficult as it may be, setting boundaries is the most effective thing you can do to change a difficult relationship. You don't need your loved one's permission to set boundaries. Once you decide something violates your boundary, you can look at your options and determine what you're willing and not willing to do in response.

Here are some examples of boundaries:

- Tom doesn't discuss issues with his wife when she starts to yell at him. He has learned to say, "I'm not going to talk with you when you're yelling at me. We'll talk later."
- Jan refuses to bring the children around her father when he's drinking.
- Jenny asked Bob to move out because he brought drugs into the house.
- Connie refused to allow her son to have pornographic materials in her home.
- Alice and Steve decided to seek custody of their two granddaughters because their daughter was not taking care of them due to her drug addiction.
- Carl refused to get between his parents in an argument. He learned to say no to requests by both of them to take sides or even to listen to their problems.
- Halley gets off the phone with her mother when she begins to feel exasperated by her. Rather than yelling at her, like before, Halley nicely ends the conversation.

Boundaries are not necessarily for your loved one. They're for you, for expressing your limits. They don't tell

him or her what to do or force change. You can't make your
loved one work, act responsible, stop an addiction, take
medication, stand up for himself or herself, admit problems, get help, talk respectfully to you, listen to you, end a
bad relationship, stop being physically or verbally abusive,
eat, not eat, take care of himself or herself, or do anything
else you want him or her to do. Your loved one chooses how
he or she wants to respond to your request. You choose your
own response accordingly.

SETTING BOUNDARIES

The following are examples of boundaries to consider:
- What you're willing to do
- What you're willing to accept and tolerate
- What you'll watch and listen to
- Where you'll go
- What type of treatment you consider respectful
- What you believe and value
- What your needs and priorities are

If you don't have boundaries, you're without protection.
People can violate you in any way they choose. Strong
boundaries are needed for many reasons:
- Your loved one will know that his or her choices carry
  consequences.
- You won't enable sin.
- You and your loved ones will be protected.
- You'll respect yourself, and others will respect you.
- You'll have self-control.
- You'll be modeling boundaries for others.

When setting boundaries, you have to take many factors
into consideration. The following things will help you decide what boundaries you need to set:
- Does what you want to do encourage your loved one to
  get help or to continue destructive habits?
- Are there innocent people who need to be protected?

- Where does your responsibility start and end?
- Where does his or her responsibility start and end?
- What is your motive?
- Are you ready to follow through with what you're stating?
- How will your decision affect you? Others?
- How important is this particular issue?
- What does God think of this issue?
- What boundaries do you need for emotional, spiritual, or physical protection?

Keeping these general considerations in mind, read through some common problem areas and decide if you could benefit from setting boundaries.

Drug and Alcohol Addictions

Addicts are self-centered and immature. Putting their addiction first, they take risks that jeopardize themselves and others. Solomon warned, "Do not gaze at wine when it is red, when it sparkles in the cup, when it goes down smoothly! In the end it bites like a snake and poisons like a viper" (Prov. 23:31-32). When your loved one is not in a sober or reasonable state of mind to make wise decisions, you'll have additional decisions to make:

- Will you allow drugs or alcohol in your home?
- Will you spend time with your loved one when he or she is under the influence?
- Will you bail your loved one out of jail if arrested?
- Will you discuss issues with your loved one when he or she is under the influence?
- Will you ride in the car with your loved one at the wheel when he or she is under the influence?
- Will you buy alcohol or drugs?
- Will you leave if your loved one gets too intoxicated or belligerent?
- Will you make excuses to the family or others for irresponsible behavior?

- Will you require treatment as a condition for your support?
- If the drug or alcohol use is related to a mental illness, will you excuse it or require treatment in order to continue your support?

Debbie and John told their son they would pay for his treatment for alcoholism but would not pay the bills for his car payment, insurance, and credit card. Paula told her family they could not drink alcohol at family parties at her house. She also decided she would not bring her children to family parties where there is alcohol. Ross told his brother not to call him when he was under the influence of drugs, because he always got in an angry mood, and it was impossible to keep from arguing with him.

Sexual Impurity

You can't control what your loved one does in regard to sexual impurity, but you can control your home and your choices. You may decide that you can't support your loved one financially because of the immoral lifestyle but will still maintain a loving and respectful relationship, expressing unconditional love. Consider the following situations:

- Will you allow pornography in your home? Will you allow children to go to a relative's house where pornography is available?
- If you know a family member or friend is having an affair, will you tell his or her spouse or keep it quiet? Will you cooperate in covering up the affair? Will you confront him or her over the affair?
- If a family member had an affair with someone and is now married to that person, how will you have a relationship with both of them?
- How will you treat a family member and the live-in boyfriend or girlfriend? Will you let them sleep in the same room? Will you visit their home?

- If a female or male relative has an out-of-wedlock pregnancy, will you offer to help with the baby or let them live with you?
- Will you forgive your spouse for having an affair? Under what conditions?

June told her brother that she disagreed with his decision to live with Brittany but continued to have a relationship with both of them. Becky told her pregnant, unmarried daughter that she could live at home but that she would expect her to take care of the baby. Kayla told her dad and stepmom that she disagreed with their affair but decided that since they were married she would forgive them and have a relationship with both of them.

Money

Money problems are common in relationships with difficult people. Irresponsible spending habits, overspending on addictions, lost jobs, poor decisions, and refusal or inability to work all result in bills not being paid. Paul goes so far as to say that if a man doesn't work, he shouldn't eat (2 Thess. 3:10) and that the one who doesn't provide for his family "is worse than an unbeliever" (1 Tim. 5:8). However, in this same context, Paul talked about taking care of needy widows, parents, and grandparents, stating that their children and grandchildren should put their religion into practice by helping them rather than placing the burden on the church. However, Paul specified that they must be living upright lives in order to receive help (1 Tim. 5:3-8).

Money is always an emotional issue. It directly affects the quality of life for all involved. Resentments can run deep in many directions.

- Will you provide basic needs and/or frivolous needs?
- Is there anything your loved one can do to be self-sufficient? Do you need to help him or her to do it rather than give money?

- What are you willing to do without?
- What if your spouse disagrees?
- What if the rest of the family refuses to help?
- What conditions will you put on giving the money?
- Is giving the money loving or enabling destructive behavior?
- Will you co-sign on loans?
- Will you be able to do this with a willing spirit?
- Will you give less to church and ministry because of what you're giving here?
- What options do you have if you can't give? Can you help your loved one get help from another source?

Karen helped her mother find work she could do at home to make money to cover bills. Rick paid for extra expenses for his mom like car repairs, since she was on a fixed income, as long as she was responsible and reasonable with her money. Allen's father gambled heavily and then would not have money to pay his bills. Allen didn't pay them even when his dad was threatened with eviction.

Family Relationship Boundaries

There will be times when the needs of your family members conflict, forcing you to make choices. Anytime you use limited time, energy, and money, you're taking them away from others and yourself. Your spouse and dependent children are more important on the whole than your parents and other extended family members, but there will be times you'll need to attend to the others too. It was God's design that children grow up and start a new family unit that takes priority over the parents (Gen. 2:24). Married people need to be concerned about pleasing their mates over others (1 Cor. 7:32-35). Paul said, "If anyone does not provide for his relatives, and especially for his immediate family, he has denied the faith and is worse than an unbeliever" (1 Tim. 5:8). Jesus knew that following Him would cause breaches among family members (Matt. 10:21, 35-37). When there's a choice between being faithful to God and being faithful to a relative, you must choose God. Conflict also arises when your priorities and values differ from those of your loved one. Consider these situations:

- Will you step in to protect your spouse and children from other family members who are disrespectful and destructive?

- What will you do and not do to cover irresponsibility?

- Will you put your spouse first even if it means offending other family members who don't understand your choices?

- What rules will you require adult children living at home to follow? What are the consequences if they don't follow them?

- What boundaries will you draw in your home regarding unacceptable behavior? How will you enforce those boundaries?

- What circumstances would cause you to refuse to be around various family members?

- Will you say no when your loved ones won't understand or approve?

- Will you do things you don't want to do because your spouse or other family member wants you to?

Always state boundaries respectfully (1 Tim. 5:1), but remember that dysfunctional families don't readily accept boundaries and will most likely not understand them. You will have to think them through, knowing it's worth the negative response you may get, and then set them anyway.

Abuse

Physical abuse is physical contact motivated by anger, punishment, and control. All are clear violations of every person's right to be treated with dignity. Physical abuse also involves threats of abuse and destruction of property. Peo-

ple under the influence of drugs and alcohol and those
with mental illnesses are most likely to have problems in this
area. The following questions have to be considered:

- What will you do if it happens only once?
- What will you do if it happens when your loved one
  drinks or uses drugs?
- Will you take violent threats seriously?
- Will you call the police to protect yourself even if it will
  cause problems for your loved one? Or will you try to
  have your loved one temporarily committed in the
  case of mental illness?
- Will you accept apologies when your loved one is re-
  morseful after an incident?
- Will you refuse to argue when your loved one is angry
  or under the influence?

You'll need to decide how serious the physical threats
are and whether you're willing to protect yourself. You
don't have to tolerate threats to your safety even when
you're dealing with family members with mental illness.

Heather was afraid of John's violence when he came
home on drugs. She decided to ask him to move out. He
threatened her, so she got a restraining order. Dave got angry and destroyed things. His wife called the police and
filed a complaint. Debbie knew Billy's mental illness was getting worse. She was afraid of the possibility of his harming
himself or her. She called his doctor to find out what options she had to get help for him.

Verbal and emotional abuse can be subtle and confusing, or it can be obvious. It's common in dysfunctional relationships. Verbal and emotional abuse stem from the desire
to control and manipulate through intimidating tactics such
as the following:

- Withdrawal
- Threats

- Ridicule
- Contempt
- Accusations
- Discounting needs, feelings, and opinions
- Teasing
- Name-calling
- Ignoring
- Withholding information, approval, affection, money, or other needs
- Denying the truth or lying
- Refusing to cooperate
- Hostile anger
- Demeaning looks and stares
- Speaking in a condescending tone
- Silent treatments
- Punishment
- Threats

Abuse is damaging. It kills the spirit of the receiver by directly attacking his or her personhood and minimizing self-worth. The recipient of abuse will typically question his or her own feelings, perceptions, and thoughts, because the abuser's reality will differ. It's hard to accept that your loved one may not be operating out of good will and honesty in the relationship, so you'll often doubt yourself instead.

You may realize that you do some of the things on that list in trying to get your loved one to change or see the truth. If you do, work on changing your behavior. The following questions regarding your loved one's abusive behavior should be considered:

- Is the abuse reoccurring? How serious is it?
- Have you tried to confront your loved one to ask that it stop?
- What do you normally do in response to the abuse? Does it make the situation worse or better? What are some of your other options?

- What tones are acceptable for the abuser to use when talking with you?

You can't make an abuser stop abusing you. In fact, when you stand up and say no to abuse, the attempts to control will often intensify as your willingness to say no produces a challenge. Serious abusers often need extensive professional therapy to change. You can remove yourself anytime you're being abused.

Pam's mother was critical of her. Pam tried to please her but was never good enough. When Pam tried to talk to her mom about problems, she would call her names and blame her. Pam tried to explain herself to her mother, but she never seemed to understand. Pam learned to stop trying to explain to get her mother's approval and instead to stop participating in abusive interactions.

General Relationship Boundaries

Relationship boundaries are complicated, since each relationship is unique. Unhealthy relationships have unhealthy boundaries. Setting boundaries is part of making all your relationships healthier. The following are some additional general boundaries to consider:

- Will you get help even if others don't approve?
- How much anger will you tolerate before you withdraw from a conflict?
- What type of conflict resolution will you use to resolve conflicts?
- What changes do you need to make in yourself?
- How much interaction can you tolerate in a difficult relationship before it affects your ability to function in other areas and relationships?
- Under what circumstances would you cut off a relationship or cut down on the amount of time you spend with your loved one?
- How much time can you spend with a loved one and still treat him or her respectfully without reacting to the dysfunction in harmful ways to both of you?

- What do you need to do to take care of yourself with your difficult loved one?

It's not wrong to retreat from a difficult relationship in order to take care of yourself. You may find there are certain family members you can see only for short times. Or there may be certain family members you won't see at the same time. There may be certain topics you won't discuss or circumstances you avoid. All those compensations are reasonable when dealing with difficult people. You need to do whatever it takes to first take care of yourself, especially when it also enables you to continue the relationship rather than cut it off completely.

WAYS TO EXPRESS BOUNDARIES

The best way to set boundaries is to speak firmly, clearly, specifically, and calmly. Screaming is not convincing, because things said in anger are often empty threats. When you set new boundaries, expect your loved one to put pressure on you to back down. Difficult people don't like changes, especially if it means you aren't enabling anymore. Threats often come as a means to make you do what he or she wants. Boundaries are yours to set and don't have to be negotiable, but if you're trying to come up with a workable solution, have some possibilities in mind. Here are some ways to state your boundaries:

- "I can't do that."
- "I can't accept that."
- "I won't talk with you when you're yelling at me."
- "I don't want to be around you when you're like that."
- "Don't call me names."
- "I won't do that anymore."
- "Please leave."
- "That would be wrong for me."
- "No."

Your loved ones also have boundaries. It may be hard for you to accept their limits, but you must. You can only choose what you will do in response. You may have to work at being respectful of others' differences and give them the dignity to do what they think is right too.

Each difficult relationship is unique. It will take time for you to be able to answer the questions that pertain to you. When your boundaries are strong, you won't question them; you'll know what you can and can't tolerate and what you need to do. Boundaries are not permanent walls; they adapt as you and your loved one change. Learn to set boundaries so you can say, "The boundary lines have fallen for me in pleasant places" (Ps. 16:6).

ENTER GOD'S REST

Come to me, all you who are weary and burdened, and I will give you rest. Take my yoke upon you and learn from me, for I am gentle and humble in heart, and you will find rest for your souls. For my yoke is easy and my burden is light. —Matt. 11:28-30

N ow that you've worked through the previous nine principles and considered incorporating them into your life, it's time to turn your loved one and your life over to God and enter His rest, knowing that He will work all things for good and will complete what He has begun in you and your loved one—a good work (Rom. 8:28; Phil. 1:6).

God loves your difficult loved one even more than you do and wants him or her saved and whole. He wants your relationship to glorify Him. Let Him do His work in your loved one's life. He knows better than you what it will take to get change.

The principles you've read about are simple, yet they're not always easy to follow. Old habits take time to change, and new habits take practice. You'll learn even from your failures as you deal with your difficult loved one.

UNDERSTANDING WHY

You may never know why God allowed your loved one to suffer from these problems. It could be a result of poor decisions in the past and in the present by you or by others. It can also be no one's fault. As Jesus told the parents of the blind man, "Neither this man nor his parents sinned . . . but this happened so that the work of God might be displayed in his life" (John 9:3). Rom. 9:6-23 explains that God is sovereign and has a right to make us any way He wants in accordance with His purpose, but it's still our responsibility to do right.

Regardless of why these problems exist, it's God's purpose to use the situation for His glory by perfecting your loved one and you. God's power is made perfect in your weaknesses (2 Cor. 12:9), and He uses the weak and lowly things to confound the wise (1 Cor. 1:27).

GOD CARES

God cares about your loved one even if his or her situation is a result of willful disobedience. God doesn't punish in anger, but he disciplines for the good of His children by allowing the reaping of the natural consequences of their choices in the hope that it will produce "a harvest of righteousness and peace for those who have been trained by it" (Heb. 12:11). God's purpose is not harsh judgment but to display His mercy and redemptive power. He's glorified by the restoration and redemption of His creation, not their destruction (1 Tim. 1:12-17). The love that led God to send His Son to die is the same love He has for you and your loved one now.

God cares about your pain too. "The LORD is close to the brokenhearted and saves those who are crushed in spirit" (Ps. 34:18). When you feel disappointment and sorrow, your job is to continue to trust in God's unfailing love and sovereign purpose, whether or not you understand why things happen the way they do. When you and your loved one are broken and hurting, God's heart is soft and loving toward both of you.

MAKE RESTITUTION

Restitution refers to the process of repairing the damage you've done. Regardless of what your loved one has done or is doing, you're responsible for the ways you've hurt him or her. You have to acknowledge your part in the relationship problems.

You can make restitution in several different ways: acknowledging and apologizing, repaying debts, doing nice things, or changing yourself and making better choices today. It's impossible to go back and alter the past. Your job is not to be good enough to make up for the past but to be a different person today. When you modify the way you treat people today, it shows not only an awareness of how you were wrong in the past but also your sincerity in wanting to change. Telling someone you're sorry opens the door to healing, but your actions need to continue showing that you mean it.

RISK A NEW BEGINNING

An end to the old means a change for the new. Change can be challenging, but it's good. When you change the way you relate to your loved one and the related difficult circumstances, you'll experience a new strength, a new dependence on the Lord, a new perspective, and new hope for a good future.

It's not easy to risk letting go. Truth can result in loss or change in a relationship. A difficult loved one may be uncomfortable with your honesty and healthful choices. It's his or her choice to decide how to respond. Most have to hit a bottom before they're willing to change. Watching your loved one hit that bottom may be one of the hardest things you've ever done. Stand firm, and let God work in his or her life. Take one day at a time.

Change is a process that takes time. You must first become aware of the need to change and then slowly begin the process. Even when you want to change, you may continue to fall back into negative old behavior. Be patient with yourself and others.

ACCEPT REALITY

One of the best ways to enter God's rest is to reach a point at which you truly surrender your hopes and desires. Each of us has dreams about how we want life to be. If you're struggling with acceptance, it's because your dreams have not been realized. Could it be that you believed your dreams were God's promises to you? Do you believe you should have what you want because you could have it if others did what you want them to do? If you do, you'll become disillusioned with God when your dreams don't come true. You must accept that your life, your loved one, and the relationship are not what you want and may not ever be. Accept the fact that you can't make up for the things missing in your loved one's life. Once you do that, you're free to decide what you'll do with the possibilities you have.

Once you accept the reality of your life and your loved one's life, you're free to make choices. When you know you have choices rather than being stuck, you can approach the relationship in an entirely different way. You accept your situation, learn to take care of yourself in it, take responsibility for your choices, and give your loved one the dignity and freedom to make his or her choices. If you accept the fact that God in His perfect wisdom has allowed your loved one's life and your life to be at this point, you can rest, give it to Him, and trust Him to use it for your good and His glory.

LIVE FOR TODAY

The easiest way to enter God's rest is to live one day at a time. That one chunk of time is manageable with God's strength, even though it isn't always easy. But you can't handle the weight of the past and future on top of that one day.

Jesus knew this. He told us in the Sermon on the Mount not to worry about material things and the future. He said, "Do not worry about tomorrow, for tomorrow will worry about itself. Each day has enough trouble of its own" (Matt.

6:34). You don't know what the future will bring. Truthfully, all of us live life one moment at a time anyway. If you focus on living that moment to the best of your ability, your tomorrows will be better.

LET OTHERS TAKE CARE OF THEMSELVES

What if your loved one makes a change and then regresses or gets worse? You can't allow these and other fears to rule your life. It's not your responsibility to make sure your loved one stays sober or clean, handles his or her relationships, gets help, takes medication, goes to church, gets treatment, goes to counseling, ends a relationship, or maintains any other change. It's no more your job to do that than it was your job to change him or her in the first place. Don't manage his or her life, check up on him or her, or ask him or her to report to you. It's his or her job to change and to maintain that change—whatever it takes. You're not the counselor, teacher, mentor, god, or doctor. You can share your feelings about the situation or ask reasonable questions; it's the obsession of finding out whether or not your loved one is doing what needs to be done that you need to let go of.

On the other hand, don't pretend things aren't happening that really *are* happening. Admit the truth to yourself. Don't allow yourself to be blind to warning signs. But know that you'll be able to deal with whatever happens because you're not in the same place you were before. You know now that you have choices and control over your own life.

REBUILD TRUST SLOWLY

Trust is not destroyed or rebuilt over night. It's destroyed through many disappointments, lies, and inconsistencies. It may be wise for you not to trust your loved one. In the past, you may have accepted a meager promise to change and jumped in with all your mind, spirit, resources, and emotions with little concern for your emotional, spiritual, or physical safety. You may have found yourself desperately disappointed when the change didn't last. In order to use wisdom, you have to allow your loved one to build a track record that merits your trust. Start slowly. Establish openness if possible so you can talk about your fears and concerns as they surface. Ask your loved one to make a commitment to honesty so that you can discuss your struggles as trust is rebuilt. In some cases this may not be appropriate and you'll have to do it on your own.

Trust is a two-way street. Your loved one may not trust you if you've been emotionally inconsistent, reactive, accusatory, angry, controlling, and hurtful even if it was out of good intentions. Even though you've changed, your loved one may react to you as though you've not changed. That may be difficult for you to endure as you may feel hurt, disappointed, and desperate to heal the wounded relationship. Continue to build a track record of consistency so your loved one can trust you to listen to him or her, allow him or her to make decisions without your interference, give unconditional love, and be emotionally consistent. It will take time.

The best way to begin is to start spending time together. When Jacob and Laban restored their strained relationship, they ate together and reaffirmed their oath to each other (Gen. 31:53-54). Eating meals together was a sign of friendship. Do things together that can build a relationship even if all the feelings and past issues aren't yet worked through.

HEAL PAST WOUNDS

It's possible to heal from almost anything if two people are willing to do the work, but it takes time, courage, and openness. It's not an easy process or one that always goes smoothly.

If your loved one has resentments and hurts caused by

you, be willing to give him or her the time and space needed to work through them. You can't force anyone to be ready on your timetable. Be willing to listen to the pain without trying to fix it. You can be most supportive by listening empathetically without arguing about differences of opinion. When you show your support, your loved one will feel loved.

It's freeing to be able to discuss your past hurts with the person who hurt you, but it's not reasonable to go back and resolve everything in your past. Your loved one may feel sorrow over what he or she did and may even be willing to change but may not be able to give you the specifics that you would like to hear.

Your loved one won't be everything you want him or her to be, nor will you be everything he or she wants you to be, even after the major problems are resolved. Acceptance of each other as you are, imperfect people who disappoint each other, is healing to both of you.

When bad memories surface, use the principles of Phil. 4:8 to think about what is true, noble, right, pure, lovely, admirable, praiseworthy, and excellent. Use the memory to thank God for how far He has brought you and the good that has come from bad, as with Joseph, who said, "You intended to harm me, but God intended it for good to accomplish what is now being done" (Gen. 50:20). Taking that perspective over all the negative things your loved one has done allows you to fully heal, even if the relationship with your loved one doesn't change or he or she continues to behave in destructive ways.

SURRENDER DISAPPOINTMENT

How do you handle the disappointment of your loved one continuing to do things that cause you and others pain? You submit to God, do what's right, and continue to trust God to redeem even this. He'll still restore your life and use you for His glory. He'll have compassion for you and be near to you in your brokenness. He won't abandon you or leave you alone. He'll continue to work in your loved one's life on His timetable, not yours. Difficult people will continue to be difficult until they're ready to change.

God does not hold the failures of another person, your relationship, or even your marriage over you as a life sentence of despair and brokenness. He knows the weakness of sinful people. He knows that sin-hardened hearts choose destruction. He does not hate the person; rather, He hates the brokenness and hurt that come from sin. There's still a future of hope, purpose, and restoration for you.

COMFORT OTHERS

Encouragement is used interchangeably in the Bible with "exhortation" and "comfort." They mean to come to a person's aid. One way to do that is to urge others to look to the future. You can bring comfort and hope through your experience to others who are hurting. "Praise be to the God and Father of our Lord Jesus Christ, the Father of compassion and the God of all comfort, who comforts us in all our troubles, so that we can comfort those in any trouble with the comfort we ourselves have received from God" (2 Cor. 1:3-4) "Therefore encourage one another and build each other up, just as in fact you are doing" (1 Thess. 5:11). The best support comes from those that have been through similar circumstances. Reach out and help others.

God is in the business of restoration. There are millions of others in difficult relationships hurting, broken, and confused, some within your circle of contact right now. When you're willing to reach out and be used, God will give you the opportunity. When you let God use your pain to help others, you'll understand His redemptive purpose in your life and be able to rejoice.

Rejoice over Redemption

"The LORD works out everything for his own ends—even the wicked for a day of disaster" (Prov. 16:4). God redeems and restores even when you make bad choices that affect your life and the lives of others. When your loved one causes you and others to bear the effects of his or her bad choices, God brings glory to himself in the process. His purpose is to restore you to himself, sanctify you, and mold you into the image of His Son to show the world His love and salvation. When you take all that life has to offer you, good and bad, and allow God to use it to mold you into His image in the midst of your difficult circumstances and then use you, you're fulfilling God's wonderful purpose for your life.

I watched every dream and hope I had die: the dream of a Christian home, the dream of serving God in a ministry with my talents, the dream of raising my daughters to be strong, healthy young women with a heart for God, and the dream of a good marriage. I also watched God restore those broken dreams and can now rejoice in His redemption.

God has a promise of restoration for you: "'I know the plans I have for you,' declares the LORD, 'plans to prosper you and not to harm you, plans to give you hope and a future'" (Jer. 29:11). Regardless of the way your relationship with your loved one goes, you have a Heavenly Father who loves you and wants to bless you. You don't have the guarantee of a perfect ending but of a life with ample provision and grace from a God who loves you enough to have sent His Son to die for you.

Isa. 61:2-4 says that Jesus has been sent "to comfort all who mourn, and provide for those who grieve in Zion—to bestow on them a crown of beauty instead of ashes, the oil of gladness instead of mourning, and a garment of praise instead of a spirit of despair. They will be called oaks of righteousness, a planting of the LORD for the display of his splendor. They will rebuild the ancient ruins and restore the places long devastated; they will renew the ruined cities that have been devastated for generations."

How will it all turn out? I don't know, and neither do you. Your hopes are just as strong as your fears, but God "is able to do immeasurably more than all we ask or imagine, according to his power that is at work within us" (Eph. 3:20).

Trust God that the minute details of your life—the mistakes, failings, imperfect people, hurts, and sins—are being woven into a beautiful tapestry (Rom. 8:28). When you reach the end of your life, you'll look back and see God's hand and know that He has molded you and accomplished His purpose in you—even in your difficult relationship.